BRIDGEPORT PUBLIC LIBRARY

DATE DUE

JUN 10 1997
FEB 16 1999
APR 9 - 1999
APR 29 1999
DEC 14 2002
JUL 09 2008
MAY 05 2010

Demco, Inc. 38-293

GREAT MYSTERIES

The Shroud of Turin

OPPOSING VIEWPOINTS®

by Daniel C. Scavone

Greenhaven Press, Inc. San Diego, California

No part of this book may be reproduced or used in any form or by any means, electrical, mechanical, or otherwise, including but not limited to photocopy, recording, or any information storage and retrieval system, without prior written permission from the publisher.

j232.966
(1)

Library of Congress Cataloging-in-Publication Data

Scavone, Daniel, 1934-

The shroud of Turin.

(Great mysteries)
Bibliography: p.
Includes index.
Summary: Explores the scientific and historic theories regarding the authenticity of the Shroud of Turin as the burial cloth of Jesus.
1. Holy Shroud—Juvenile literature. [1. Holy Shroud] I. Title. II. Series: Great mysteries (Saint Paul, Minn.)
BT587.S4S27 1989 232.9'66 88-24355
ISBN 0-89908-061-8

© Copyright 1989 by Greenhaven Press, Inc.
Every effort has been made to trace owners of copyright material.

To my children
D.J.S. and C.B.S.
and to two true friends
C.O.H. and B.J.M.

Thanks to friends and associates who have given me support by viewing my research on The Shroud with benign confidence, and especially to Carolyn Hoos, who read and made important corrections to the manuscript; to the University of Southern Indiana for making available its many scholarly resources; to Father Adam Otterbein for the generous gift of his time and the use of the Wuenschel collection; to Bonnie Szumski, my editor, who helped make this book better than it would have been, by challenging the text throughout for clarity.

Contents

Introduction

"Penetrating so many secrets, we cease to believe in the unknowable. But there it sits nevertheless, calmly licking its chops."

H.L. Mencken, American essayist

This book is written for the curious—those who want to explore the mysteries that are everywhere. To be human is to be constantly surrounded by wonderment. How do birds fly? Are ghosts real? Can animals and people communicate? Was King Arthur a real person or a myth? Why did Amelia Earhart disappear? Did history really happen the way we think it did? Where did the world come from? Where is it going?

Great Mysteries: Opposing Viewpoints books are intended to offer the reader an opportunity to explore some of the many mysteries that both trouble and intrigue us. For the span of each book, we want the reader to feel that he or she is a scientist investigating the extinction of the dinosaurs, an archaeologist searching for clues to the origin of the great Egyptian pyramids, a psychic detective testing the existence of ESP.

One thing all mysteries have in common is that there is no ready answer. Often there are *many* answers but none on which even the majority of authorities agrees. *Great Mysteries: Opposing Viewpoints* books introduce the intriguing views of the experts, allowing the reader to participate in their explorations, their theories, and their disagreements as they try to explain the mysteries of our world.

But most readers won't want to stop here. These *Great Mysteries: Opposing Viewpoints* aim to stimulate the reader's curiosity. Although truth is often impossible to discover, the search is fascinating. It is up to the reader to examine the evidence, to decide whether the answer is there—or to explore further.

Preface

What Is the Turin Shroud?

In the summer of 1978 three million tourists visited Torino (Turin), Italy. They had come from all over the world to wait in line and to look upon a linen cloth which had been in Turin for more than four hundred years. They knew that the cloth had not been shown to the general public for almost fifty years and that this would likely be its only display in their lifetime. As they entered the cathedral of St. John the Baptist they could see a large, narrow cloth measuring 14.3 feet long by 3.5 feet wide. It was flood-lit and was mounted in front of the main altar at the far end of the church. Gradually, as they neared the altar, they began to notice on the cloth an extremely faint, reddish-colored, life-sized image of a bearded man. The man looked strikingly like traditional images of Jesus Christ. Indeed, the cloth known as the Shroud of Turin is thought by many people to be the actual burial wrapping of Jesus.

Both the front and the back of the body can be seen on the cloth. From either end the figure appears feet-head, head-feet. This tells us that he may have been placed on one half of the cloth. The other half would then have been pulled over the front of the body.

Opposite page: Cathedral of St. John the Baptist in Turin, Italy. A baroque dome in which the Shroud is locked was added to the old church in the 17th century.

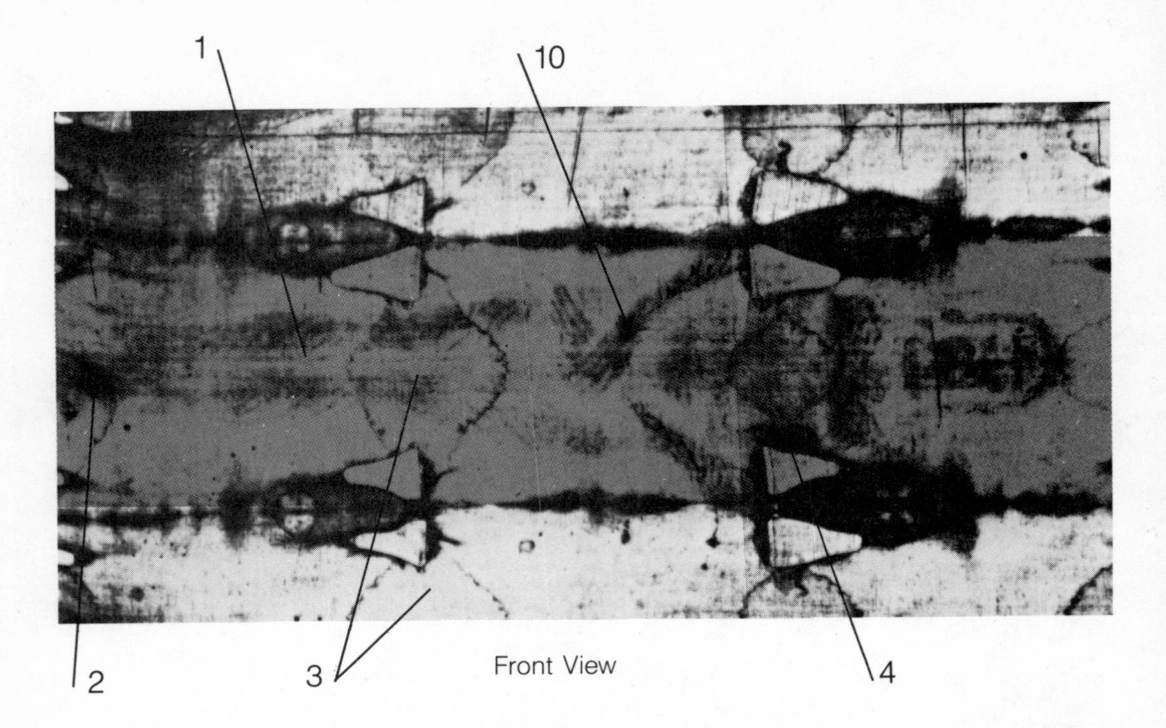

Front View

1. Image of a naked man, foot to head and head to foot.
2. Blood from nail wound in foot.
3. Stains from water used to extinguish 1532 fire.
4. Blood from side wound.
5. Scourge marks from flagrum.
6. Blood at heel and sole of right foot.

There are stains on the body that resemble blood stains from an ancient Roman scourging and crucifixion with nails. On the front, there are trickles of blood on the man's forehead, a large stain on his right side, and stains from a wound in one wrist. (The other hand cannot be seen.) Both arms show blood runoffs from the hands to the elbows. On the back can be counted about 120 small stains which conform to the shape of a Roman whip. More blood trickles are seen on the back of the head. The feet are bloodied from apparent nail wounds.

In short, the wounds on the image of the Shroud conform to the story of Jesus' crucifixion as told in the Gospels.

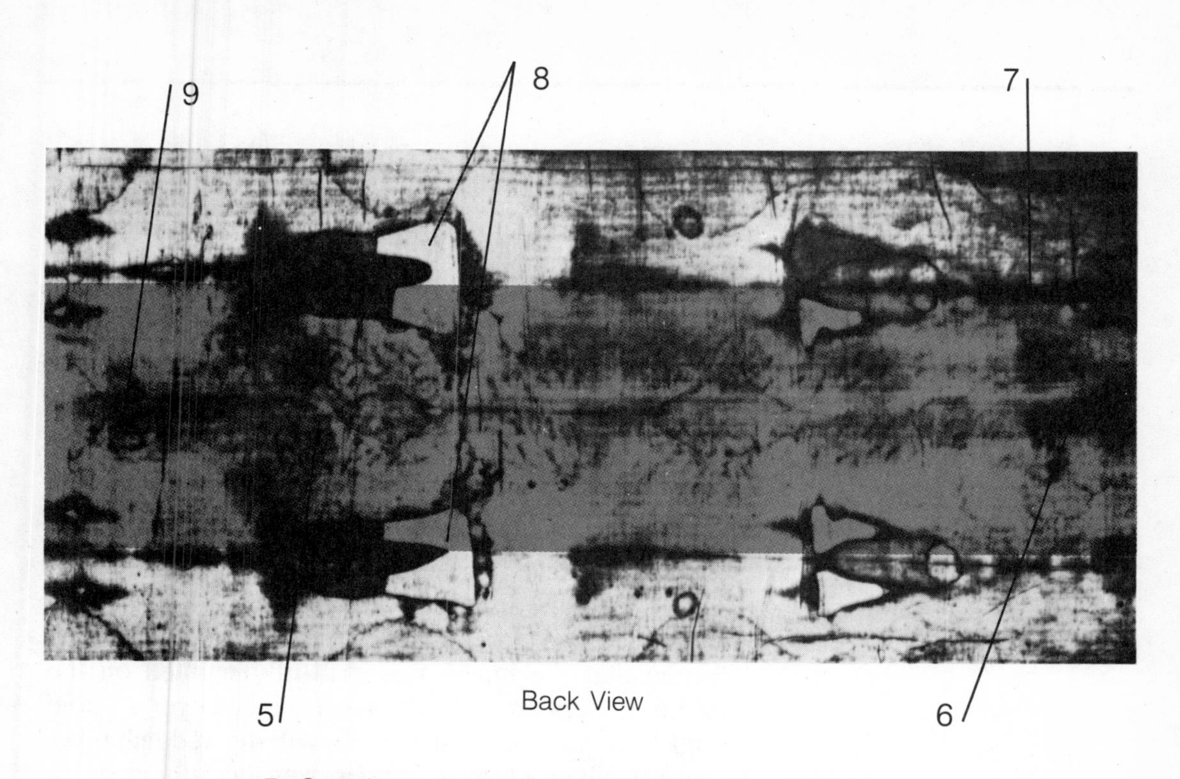

Back View

7. Scorch marks run the length of the Shroud from 1532 fire.
8. Patches covering the burn holes, sewn by Poor Clare Nuns in Chambery.
9. Blood on forehead and back of head caused by the crown of thorns.
10. Nail wound on the left wrist.

There are other visible marks. The Shroud has two long burn lines running down its whole length. It has fourteen triangle-shaped patches covering burn holes. There are also several diamond-shaped water marks. The cause of these marks is well known: The Shroud was once damaged in a fire in Chambery, France, in the year 1532.

Finally, along one whole side, a strip of linen cloth has been sewn on. We do not know when, why, or by whom this side-strip was added to the Shroud. But remember this side-strip for it will become an important clue as we try to unravel the mystery of the Turin Shroud.

The name of Jesus Christ is known all over the world. He is one of history's great religious leaders, along with Mohammed, the Buddha, Confucius, and Moses. Our knowledge of Jesus has been based almost solely on the stories in the Bible. He wrote no books himself, and there were no statues or coins commemorating his physical appearance. The Gospels say almost nothing about what Jesus looked like. In fact, if the Shroud of Turin is genuine, it may be the one surviving original portrait of Jesus.

Because the Shroud markings correspond perfectly to the story of Jesus' death in the Gospels, many scholars believe it is the burial wrapping of Jesus. But other scholars disagree. They think the Shroud was fashioned by a clever artist around the year 1350. Some argue that the image was skillfully painted on the cloth. Others think the cloth was placed over a statue and the image was brushed on with dry reddish powder (as when you place paper over a coin and rub it with the side of a pencil point). Then the "bloodstains" were painted on. This might have been done, they argue, as a religious hoax to fool pilgrims out of their money, or the artist might have had a sincere religious motive.

This is the subject of this book: Is the Turin Shroud the sheet which, as we read in the Bible, Joseph of Arimathea bought to place over the corpse of Jesus on the first Good Friday? Or is it an artistic creation of the Middle Ages? Is it about 2000 years old or does it go back only 630 years (to about the year 1355)?

Many Experts Have Studied the Shroud

In our attempt to solve this mystery, we must turn to the work of many different types of experts. Each expert has studied only his own special part of the mystery of the Shroud. Chemists have investigated only the chemical aspects. Palynologists (pollen experts) have investigated the pollens found among the fibers of the cloth. Historians have searched for historical records from early centuries to see if they can prove whether the Shroud is ancient (from the time of Christ) or medieval (about 1355). Criminologists, pathologists (who examine dead bodies), and hematologists (blood specialists) are also working on the mystery of the Shroud.

Each specialist has tried to solve a set of mini-mysteries in order to contribute to the solution of the ultimate mystery—whether the Shroud is or is not the burial wrapping of Jesus Christ, the most important religious figure in the western world.

In several areas the specialists themselves have disagreed. They have inspected the same set of facts but have reached opposing conclusions. The only thing everyone agrees on is that the mystery of the Shroud continues to be an exciting puzzle.

"No picture in our museums, no sacred image in our churches has ever portrayed more impressively the likeness of what we think was the Christ of the Gospels."

Joe Luis Carreno, *Shroud of Christ*

"There is no clue to the physical appearance of Jesus in the gospels or, for that matter, anywhere in the New Testament."

Author Joe Nickell, *Inquest on the Shroud of Turin*

One

The Shroud Appears and the Mystery Begins

The mystery surrounding the Shroud began in the year 1389. That year, the Bishop of Troyes in France, wrote a long letter to Pope Clement VII, at that time the leader of all Christians. The Bishop, Pierre d'Arcis, complained in this letter that a knight named Geoffroy de Charny (whom we will call Geoffroy II) had placed a large cloth in his local church in Lirey, France. Geoffroy II was claiming that the cloth was Jesus' burial cloth and that the image on it was that of Jesus' crucified body.

Many people, d'Arcis continued, were visiting the church to see this sheet, and they were making donations. He charged that Geoffroy II was doing this for money. Though Bishop d'Arcis had not seen the cloth, he thought it could not be the actual cloth which had covered Jesus' body because the Bible does not mention an image on the shroud of Jesus. He was also angry because Geoffroy had not asked his permission to display the cloth, but had gone over his head directly to the Pope's representatives. He had gotten permission from them.

The letter went on to say that "about 34 years ago" Geoffroy's father (whom we shall call Geoffroy I),

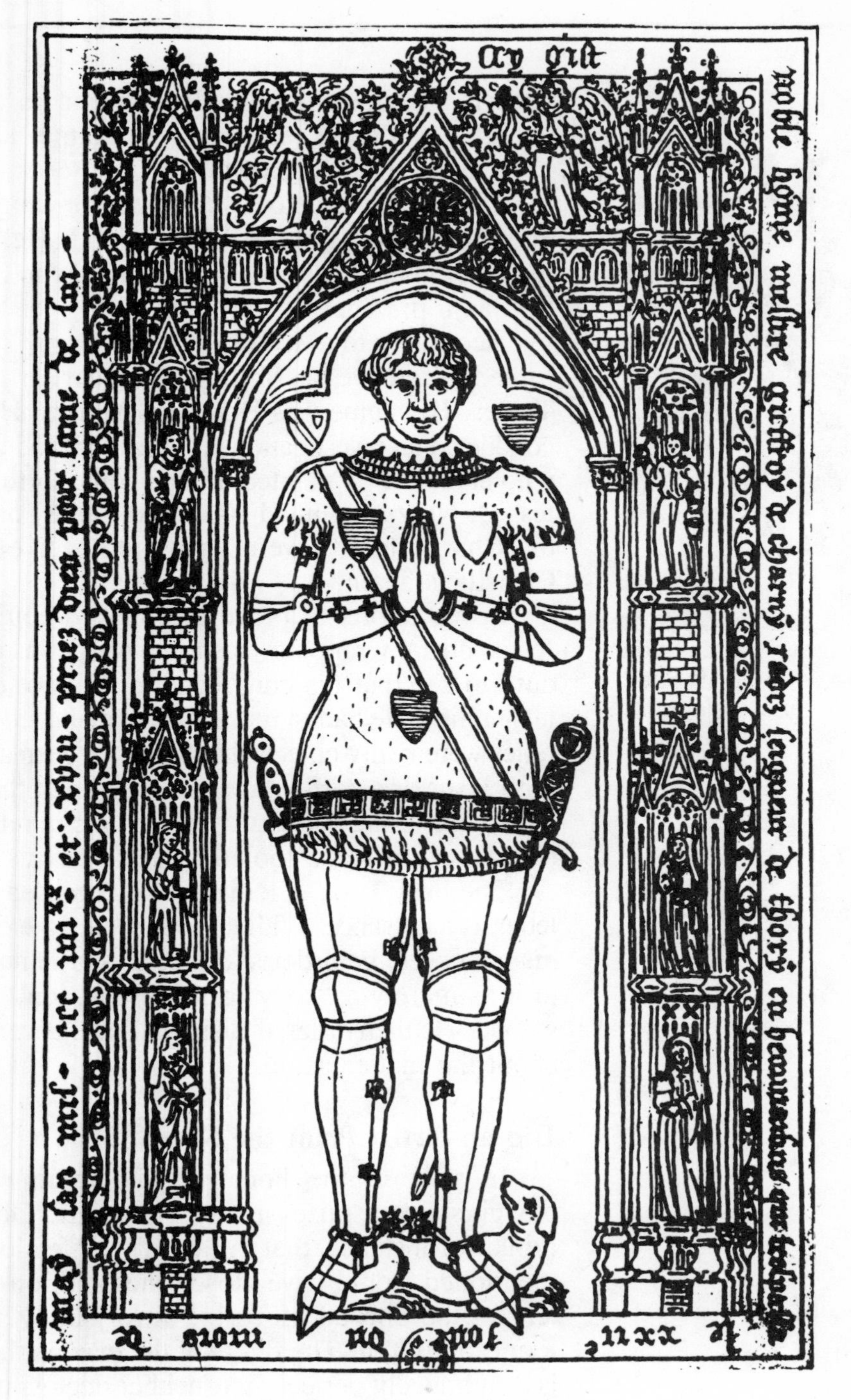

Geoffroy II de Charny, taken
from a tombstone.

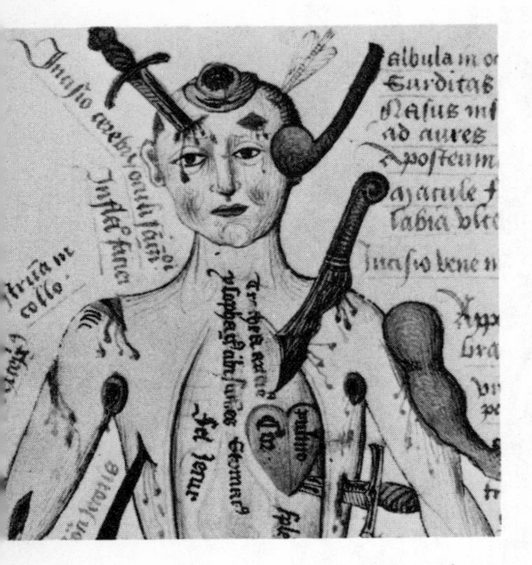

"Wound-man" is taken from a 15th century book on anatomy and illustrates how little medieval artists knew about bleeding.

had first placed the so-called Shroud in the Lirey church. "About 34 years ago" would mean about the year 1355, since Bishop d'Arcis's letter was written in 1389. This Geoffroy was a warrior-knight in the Hundred Years' War against England. He had built the Lirey church because of a vow made in 1342 while he was a prisoner of the British.

According to d'Arcis's letter, Geoffroy I had been forced to remove his Shroud by an earlier Bishop of Troyes. His name was Henry of Poitiers. Henry had conducted an investigation around 1355, and the "artist who had cleverly painted it" had come forth and confessed. Now, continued d'Arcis, the Lirey priests and the Charny family were trying to deceive the poor Christians again.

In his efforts to prove the Shroud could not be Jesus' burial wrapping, Bishop d'Arcis was doing his duty to see that his congregation was not duped by false relics. He had to make sure that alleged religious relics were really objects that had once been associated with Jesus or a particular saint. People of the Middle Ages held strong beliefs in miracles and in relics. They could too easily be fooled by false claims.

The busy Pope, Clement VII, regarded d'Arcis's letter as a nuisance. Without ever seeing the cloth with his own eyes, he ordered the priests at Lirey to refer to it as merely a "copy or representation" of Jesus' shroud. He then ordered Bishop d'Arcis never to speak about the matter again.

Did an Artist Paint the Shroud?

In spite of the Pope's casual treatment of it, d'Arcis's letter raises many questions. One would think, for instance, that the artist's confession d'Arcis mentioned would have closed the book on the mystery of the Shroud of Turin. Surprisingly, however, it only adds to it: The figure of the man on the Shroud is anatomically perfect. Yet, neither doctors nor artists of the period around 1355 knew enough about the human body to represent it so perfectly. As we will see later, the flows of blood on the Shroud man are natural and accurate. From numerous paintings we know that artists of that time did not know how to depict realistic bleeding. Also, the figure is naked, but artists of that time normally did not show the human body naked. And Jesus was never depicted unclothed.

Who, then, was this genius who was so original as to be the first to draw the human body nude and was so far ahead of his time in his knowledge of human anatomy? Bishop d'Arcis did not name him. Shouldn't he have been well known?

Next, d'Arcis's phrase "about 34 years ago," raises questions. Apparently he did not have an official dated document before him. His letter frequently used the expressions "it is reported" or "they say." His information was mostly hearsay evidence.

What documents, records, or other evidence do we have today of Bishop Henry's supposed investigation of 1355 ("about 34 years ago")? None. Today only one letter exists from Bishop Henry to Geoffroy I, first owner of the Shroud. In this letter Bishop Henry

Medallion found in the Seine River showing the twin image of the Shroud above two family crests, that of the Charny family and that of the Vergy family. It dates from between 1357 and 1389. These medals may have been souvenirs issued or sold to pilgrims who visited the Shroud at Lirey church.

Shroud chapel at Chambery, France.

is not angry and he is not suspicious. Its date is May 28, 1356. So it was written just about the time when he was supposed to be accusing Geoffroy of displaying a false relic. Yet the letter praises and blesses Geoffroy I for his work in promoting the Christian faith. There is no reference at all to the Shroud or to any investigation.

One thing is certain, there is only one person who could have cleared up this portion of the Shroud's mystery: Geoffroy I himself. Geoffroy I has been called "the Perfect Knight." His life was one of service to king and country. Knights swore an oath to their feudal lord or king that they would serve on command. In return they received a fief, or land, from their lord. Geoffroy's life is studded with military service. The Hundred Years' War was a life-and-death struggle for France. Geoffroy performed honorably for his country.

Geoffroy's honorable service earned him the title of *porte-oriflamme* of France. This means he rode next to King John the Good in battle carrying the royal standard or pennant. He met his death when he threw himself in the path of a lance aimed at his king. Geoffroy I would surely have told the truth about the Shroud. What truth would he have told?

Geoffroy II claimed that his father had received the Shroud as a gift for his valor in war. Geoffroy II's daughter, Marguerite, the last of the Charnys to own the Shroud, said her grandfather (Geoffroy I) won it in battle. These vague statements have become part of the mystery of the Shroud. But since they are the only record we have of how Geoffroy I received the Shroud, they are important.

Unfortunately, Geoffroy I died in battle without telling anyone how or when he had acquired the Shroud. In fact, Geoffroy I never spoke of having the Shroud! We only know he had it from Bishop d'Arcis's letter and from the claims of his son, Geoffroy II, and his granddaughter Marguerite.

Geoffroy I's silence suggests another possibility. Perhaps Jeanne de Vergy, Geoffroy's widow, began to promote the Shroud in the Lirey church after Geoffroy's death. Souvenir medals of the Shroud from the fourteenth century have the image of the Shroud man and are also stamped with the Charny family crest and the family crest of Jeanne de Vergy. If it was Jeanne and not Geoffroy I who first publicized the Shroud, this could explain why Henry's letter to Geoffroy I never mentions the Shroud.

Rest of Shroud's History Well-Known

The Shroud's history since d'Arcis's letter is well known. After Jeanne's death, the Shroud was owned by Marguerite de Charny, the daughter of Geoffroy II. By 1452 Marguerite de Charny had fallen on hard

"About 34 years ago [1355-1356] . . . after diligent inquiry and examination, [Henry of Poitiers, Bishop of Troyes] discovered the fraud and how said cloth had been cunningly painted, the truth being attested by the artist who had painted it, to wit, that it was the work of human skill and not miraculously made."

Memorandum of Pierre d'Arcis, Bishop of Troyes, to Pope Clement VII, 1389

"Any painter who were ever to try to portray a face of the dead Christ with all the marks left on it by the savage treatment inflicted on the Christ of the Gospels, would only end up with a monstrous-looking portrait. All of those marks are visible on the incomparable face of the man of the Shroud, and I wish I had been the artist who portrayed it. I could not have done it in any case. No artist could, not certainly by painting a negative as the Shroud forger supposedly did."

Vice president of the USA Holy Shroud Guild, Father Peter Rinaldi

times, so she traded the Shroud to Duke Louis of Savoy. In return she received some land on which she could collect rent.

The Shroud was then sent by Duke Louis to his Savoy residence at Chambery, France, and was placed in the cathedral there. In 1532 a fire destroyed the cathedral and damaged the Shroud. We can still see these burn marks on the Shroud today. In 1578 the Savoys took the Shroud across the Alps to Torino, Italy. This city became the new Savoy capital. In a few years the Shroud was placed in a fine new baroque chapel attached to Turin's ancient cathedral of St. John the Baptist. The chapel is called the Capella Royale or "Royal Chapel." The Shroud has remained there until this present day.

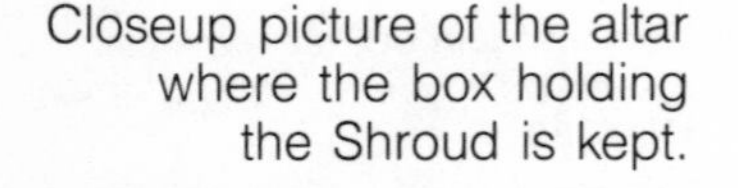

Closeup picture of the altar where the box holding the Shroud is kept.

It is seldom taken out of its bejewelled box. Inside the box the Shroud is rolled up on a satin-lined roller. The box is sealed inside a lead case and is kept locked inside a niche behind the altar of the Holy Chapel. The Capella Santa is separated from the older cathedral by a great iron gate which is also kept locked.

The Shroud has been removed from its secure niche only about twice each century since 1578. Its last public showing was in 1978, the 400th anniversary of its arrival in Turin.

Is the Shroud Authentic?

So far we know that the earliest documented evidence scholars have found about the Shroud is Bishop d'Arcis's letter in which he claims the Shroud is a fake. Remember, however, that he based his opinion on two things: a hearsay report that an artist confessed to painting the Shroud and the fact that the Bible says nothing about Jesus' burial sheet having an image. The Bishop concluded the Shroud at Lirey must have been a recent painting. It seems like a logical conclusion. But the Bishop's opinion has not remained unchallenged.

"[The image] is not the product of an artist."

STURP, Summary of Official Statement

"Since an artist might well have bothered to obtain ancient linen, a date of even 30 AD, plus or minus 100 years (70 BC—130 AD) could not rule out forgery."

Research physicist Marvin Mueller, Los Alamos National Laboratory

Two

The Shroud Is Photographed

In 1898 a decision was made which would bring the Shroud face to face with modern science. The decision was made to photograph the Shroud for the first time! Photographs would preserve the appearance of the Shroud in case of loss or damage. Remember that very few living people had ever seen the Shroud and drawings of it were quite poor. The Shroud had last been displayed publicly in 1868. Only those who were in Turin at that time had seen it. Photographs could be reproduced in books and magazines. The world could at last view what many believed was an image of the face and body of Jesus himself!

An amateur photographer, Secondo Pia, was chosen to take the first pictures of the Shroud. They would be in black and white since color photography was not commonly used at the time. The image of the man on the Shroud was extremely faint. Would it show up in the picture? Pia wondered more than anyone else. He recorded his surprise—his astonishment—when he began to see the results of his work in the developing tray. The faint, almost ghostlike image now appeared in reverse on his negative. In this form the image took on a new realism. He felt he was

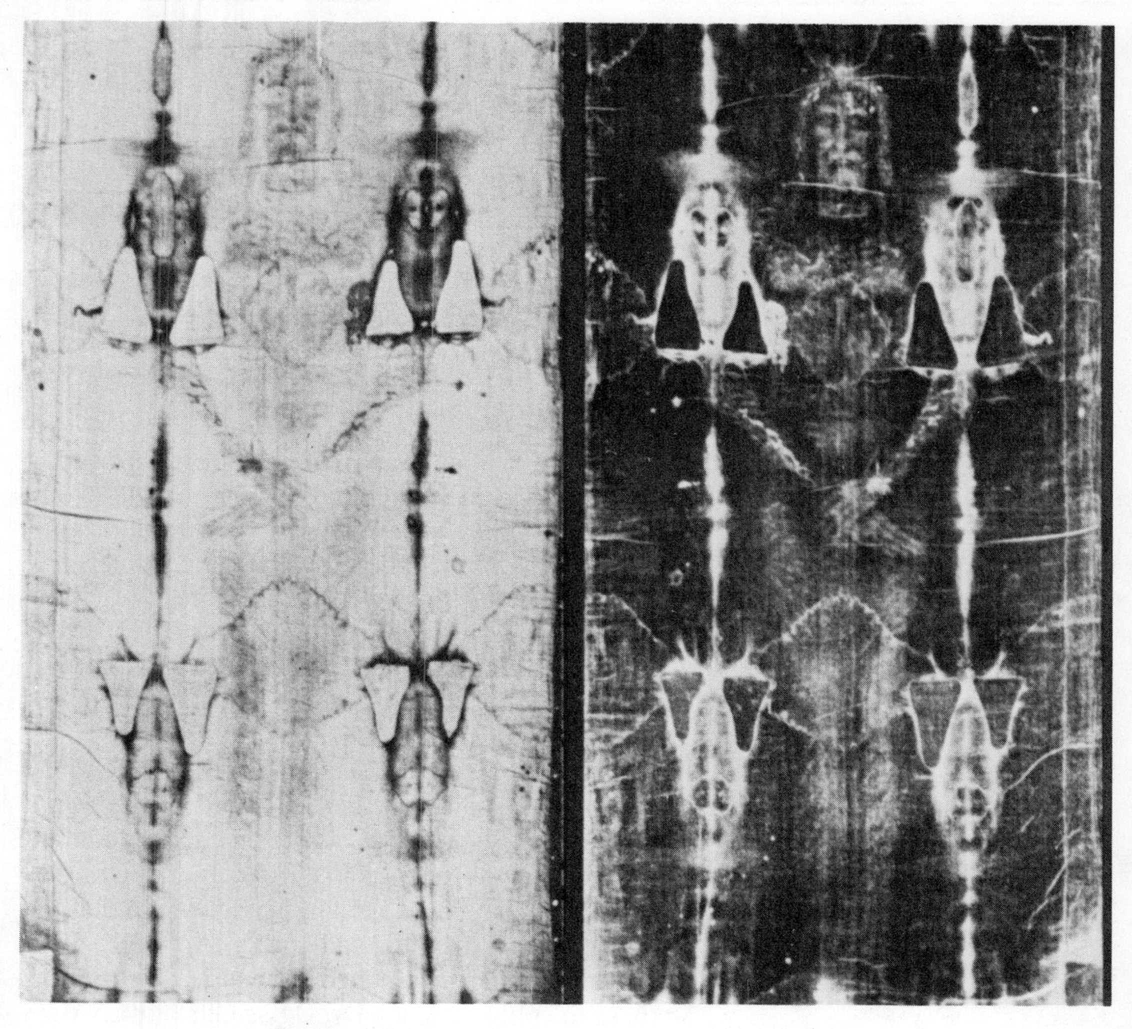

Positive and negative photographs of the Shroud
taken by Giuseppe Enrie.

Secondo Pia in 1898, first person to photograph the Shroud.

looking upon the face of the Savior himself as He appeared in death in the tomb.

Today, we too can see how realistic the negative of the Shroud looks. In fact, the Shroud itself looks like a photographic negative. Some Shroud scholars, in their desire to figure out the cause of the image, have wondered if the Shroud's linen could somehow have been "sensitized," as special photographic paper is, so that it can receive photographic images.

The Turn-of-the-Century Debate, 1898-1912

These first photographs of the Shroud proved to be a turning point in the study of the famous cloth. They seemed to offer scientific support to the claims that the Shroud was authentic. After all, the negative had given the world a more lifelike image of Christ than anyone had ever hoped for. Consequently, the authorities in Turin who have the say-so in what happens to the Shroud became less hostile to the old "enemy," science.

As a result of the photos, the Shroud came to the attention of the scientific world. Dr. Paul Vignon, a French scientist who had been interested in the Shroud for several years, brought it to the attention of Dr. Yves Delage, president of the French Academy of Sciences.

Secondo Pia's original glass negative held by Reverend Piero Coero-Borga.

At a meeting of the Academy on April 21, 1902, Dr. Delage presented a paper giving the results of his study of the photos. Since Dr. Delage had always been a skeptic and an agnostic, everyone expected him to denounce the Shroud as a worthless hoax. The audience of his fellow scientists was astounded to hear what this man of science believed. He claimed that the Shroud was probably the actual burial wrapping of Christ described in the Bible. Many in the audience of scientists were angered by Dr. Delage's conclusion. He had not, after all, performed any scientific tests on the cloth. His conclusion was based on instinct and the photos.

In the years after Delage's famous paper, a great

debate went on among scientists and historians. Some favored the genuineness of the Shroud; others denied that it could really be Jesus' burial cloth. Among the latter were two Catholic priests, one in France and one in America. They were also eminent history scholars. The first of these was Cyr Ulysses Chevalier, an expert in French history. It was he who first discovered the letter of Bishop d'Arcis, which, as we saw, condemned the Shroud as an artist's fake. The second was Reverend Herbert Thurston in the U.S. In 1912, he wrote an article on the Shroud for the *Catholic Encyclopedia,* the unofficial guidebook of the Catholic faith. In the article, Thurston presented Reverend Chevalier's arguments. Very few Catholics and indeed very few Christians believed in the Shroud after this article appeared.

For the next twenty years the Shroud lay silently in its box. For one thing, the First World War (1914-1918) distracted people from such matters. Thus, very few authors wrote about the Shroud. Anyway, hadn't it been proved to be false?

It wasn't until 1931 and again in 1933 that the Shroud was publicly shown to all who traveled to Turin to see it. In 1931 it was photographed a second time, on this occasion by Giuseppe Enrie, a professional photographer. His pictures were much clearer than Pia's and led to another breakthrough in the study of the Shroud: Paul Vignon, the Shroud investigator, was able to show from these new photos that the Shroud may very well have been the "original" for all portraits of Jesus' face. If so, it would have been used by artists long before 1350.

Dr. Paul Vignon, who first noticed similarities between traditional portraits of Jesus and the man on the Shroud.

Reverend Ulysses Chevalier called the Shroud a forgery.

Vignon: The Shroud as Possible "Original" for Jesus' Face in Art

Vignon studied the numerous artists' portraits of Jesus in churches and museums. Many of them were made much earlier than 1350. Yet, strangely, they bore a strong resemblance to the face of the man on the Shroud. In fact, Vignon was able to point out about

"Surely it is conceivable that a medieval artist could have intended to suggest that the nail had entered the upper part of the palm at an oblique angle (slanting toward the arm), thus emerging at the wrist."

Shroud Researcher Joe Nickell

"I have studied hundreds of paintings, sculptures and carvings of Christ's crucifixion and deposition, from the 13th to the 16th centuries, and not one of them shows a nail wound anywhere but in the palm of the hand."

Art historian John McNair

fifteen details found on many of the early portraits which could only be explained if the Shroud face was the model.

The most noticeable of these details are the following:

1. Almost all portraits of Jesus show two or three strands of hair in the middle of the forehead. These could be an artist's rendering of the reverse "figure 3" bloodstain on the Shroud man's forehead. What other reason would there be for artists consistently to paint in the strands of hair?

2. Many portraits of Jesus show one eyebrow higher than the other, as on the Shroud face.

3. Most intriguing of all is the fact that many portraits have a strange shape that looks like a box without

Some of the Vignon markings.
1. Reverse "3" bloodstain becomes strands of hair.
2. "Box" without a lid in cloth weave.
3. Rounded "v" below box in cloth weave.
4. Cleavage in beard.
5. Half-moon shaped bruise.
6. One eyebrow is higher than the other.
7. Swollen cheek bone.

a lid over a "v" at the bridge of the nose. This box is clearly visible in the weave of the cloth on the Shroud just above the nose.

The resemblance of Christ-portraits to the face of the Shroud man is one of the most persuasive reasons for believing that the Shroud of Turin was used by early artists. The Shroud would thus be very old and may be our original source for what Jesus looked like.

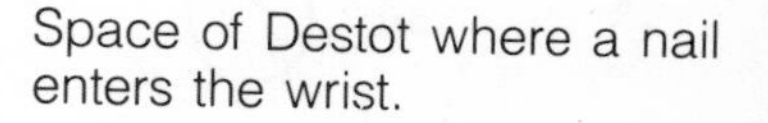

Space of Destot where a nail enters the wrist.

Barbet: The Image on the Shroud Is That of a Crucified Man

In 1950 the Shroud received another vote of confidence when a physician in France, Dr. Pierre Barbet, published his book *A Doctor at Calvary.* The book reported all that he had learned—by experiments with live and dead bodies—about the grisly subject of crucifixion.

Dr. Barbet discovered that when a person is crucified, death finally comes by suffocation or asphyxiation. While the victim is hanging by his hands, the lungs remain expanded as they are when we breathe in. The victim loses his ability to exhale. In order to regain normal breathing, the victim shifts his weight to his feet. When he does this, the angle of his arms changes slightly. Blood flowing or seeping from the nail wounds thus changes its drip-direction on the arms.

Interestingly, the seepage of blood on the arms of the Shroud man did flow in two different directions, as if he had altered his position on a cross. Barbet thought that an artist probably would not think of this detail if he was painting the "blood."

Dr. Barbet also learned that in nailing a body to a cross, the nails should go into the bony area at the base of the hand and not into the palms. In the bony area there is a point known as *the space of Destot* which will accept the nail. The bones are not broken but are spread apart against each other. The hand will be securely nailed to the wood. In contrast, the skin

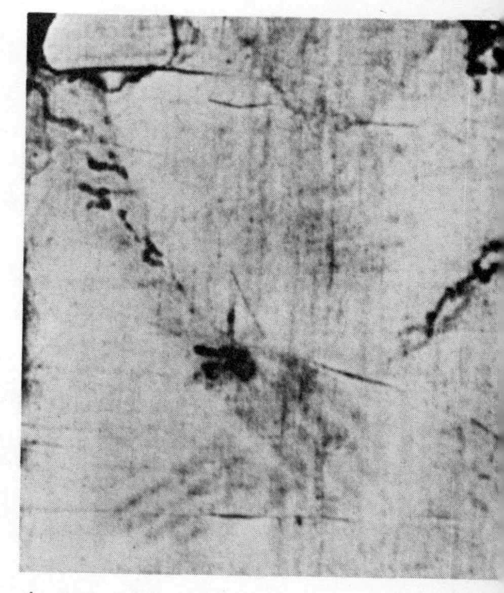

Arms and hands on the Shroud show possible blood at the wrist and flows of blood on the arms.

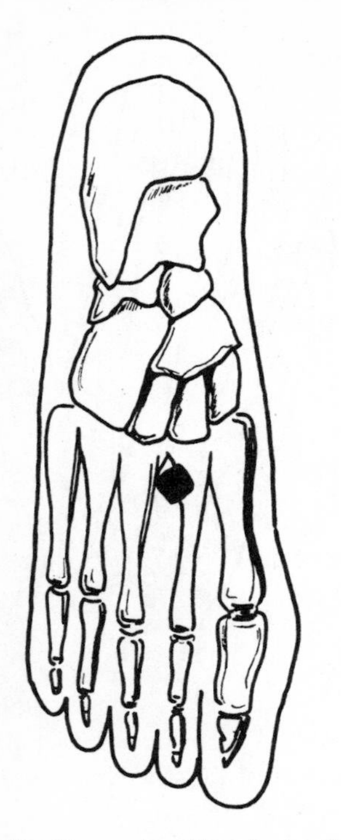

Position of nail hole in the foot of a crucifixion victim.

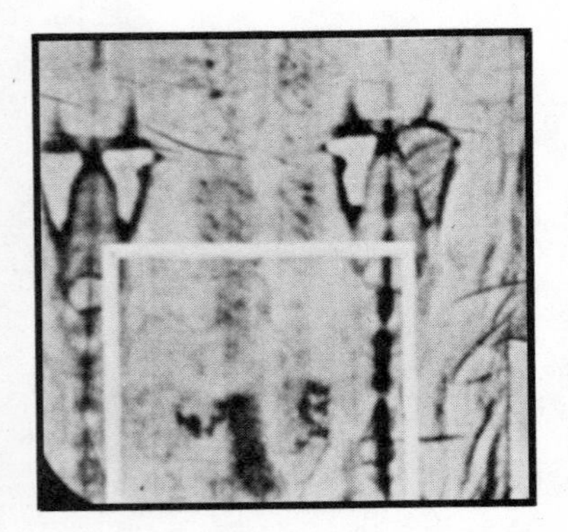

Bottom of the Shroud showing a possible bloodstain at the feet.

of the palms will tear and will not support the weight of a body. Again, the Shroud shows bloodstains in the wrist area, and not in the palms. The Shroud shows precisely the correct position of the nail in a crucifixion.

Barbet learned other things about crucifixions which are quite gruesome and which are not mentioned in the Bible. The Gospel writers were not aware of these medical facts. The first is that a nail in the wrist area will touch or cut into the median nerve of each hand. This is a large nerve and when it is touched the pain is unbearable. When this nerve is touched, it causes the thumbs to fold into the palms. Looking at the back of the hands, one does not see the thumbs. Look at the hands of the Shroud man; you will not see thumbs. Here is medical evidence that this is a real human corpse.

The same terrible pain is felt when the plantar nerves in the feet are touched. During the breathing ordeal mentioned earlier, a crucifixion victim would have to shift his weight to his feet in order to regain normal breathing. But because of the intense pain there, he would have to shift his weight back up to his hands as soon as he could again breathe normally. This would ease the pain of the nail in his feet. The position of the bloodstain in the feet of the Shroud man is exactly at a point where it would be striking the plantar nerve. The pain must have been immense.

Finally, the many dumbbell-shaped bloodstains all over the back of the body perfectly match the kind of scourge or whip used by the Romans at the time of Christ. In the ruins of Herculaneum, in Italy, which was destroyed by the eruption of Mt. Vesuvius along with Pompeii in 73 A.D., whips like the one pictured here were found. They consist of wooden handles and two or three leather thongs ending in dumbbell-shaped lead weights. These scourges would have left the type of cut which we see on the body on the Shroud. It is one of the chief reasons, so far, for believing that

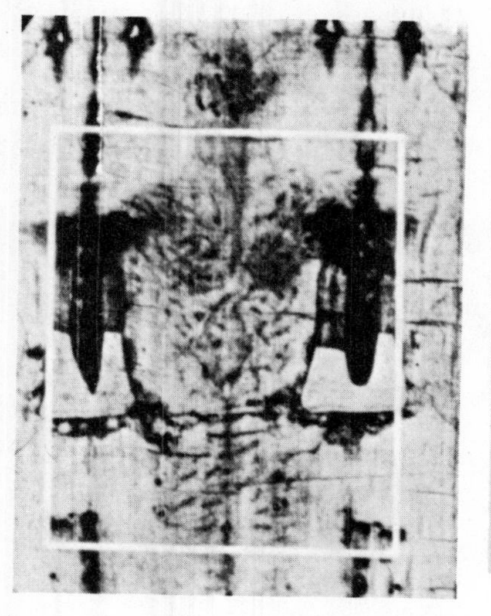

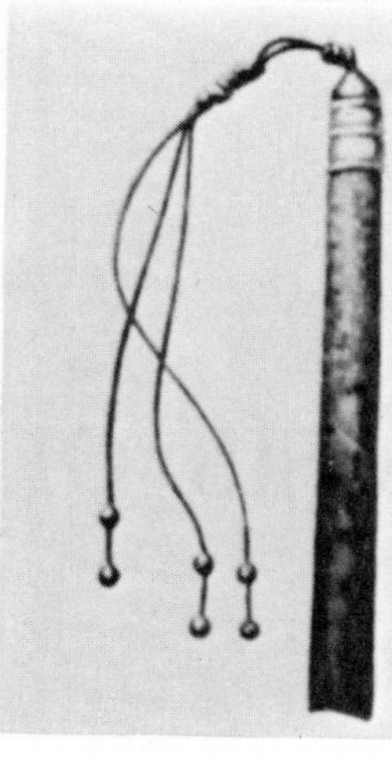

Dumbbell shaped marks on the back of the Shroud man could have been caused by the Roman whip on the right.

the Shroud represents a *Roman* crucifixion.

The whip marks on the shoulders seem to be other signs that this was a Roman crucifixion. The bloodstains there are smudged and distorted as if a heavy object had been placed on the shoulders. We know from Roman writings that crucifixion victims had to carry the cross-beam (Latin word, *patibulum*) to the crucifixion site. This is the beam to which the hands would be fastened. The vertical beam (Latin, *stipes*) was already placed in the ground at the site, usually outside the city walls. The Shroud man seems to have carried his cross in the manner of Roman crucifixions.

These bloodstains on the body of the Shroud man argue that the Shroud may have covered a real crucified corpse. The bloodstains are eloquent silent witnesses that the Turin Shroud may be very ancient and not an artist's forgery of the fourteenth century. This is so since Roman crucifixion was no longer practiced after about 330 A.D.

The conclusions of Barbet, Vignon, and Delage were based on photos of the Shroud. What would scientists find when the cloth itself was tested? Could the cloth provide us with evidence to conclude the mystery?

"If I had to go into a courtroom, I could not say there was rigor, whether the man was alive or dead, or that this picture was a true reflection of injuries to the body. In no way did I hold myself out as an expert on the shroud, but I do know dead bodies. Human bodies don't produce this kind of pattern."

Deputy Chief Medical Examiner
of Suffolk County (NY)
Michael M. Baden

"I've been involved in the invention of many complicated visual processes, and I can tell you that no one could have faked that image. No one could do it today with all the technology we have. It's a perfect negative. It has a photographic quality that is extremely precise."

British photographer Leo Valla

Three

The First Tests on the Cloth

Opposite page: A microscopic picture showing the cloth weave at the tip of the nose of the Shroud image. The dark flecks could be blood.

The idea of testing the Shroud had been unthinkable to early Christians. Of course, in earlier times there were no scientific tests which could penetrate the Shroud's mystery. Science was in its infancy. Faith had to be enough, and most people who knew of the Shroud believed in it without questioning.

But science advanced, finally, to a level where it might shed light on the riddle. By about 1890, scientists were making great strides in the fields of chemistry, physics, medicine, and photography. Microscopes and telescopes were being improved. The mysteries of outer space and of atomic particles were being solved. New facts were discovered. Many chemical elements were identified and named for the first time.

People began to think about studying the Shroud by means of science. We know of the great debate about whether an artist had made the image and bloodstains. Well, the Shroud was available. Why not see if there was paint or other artists' colors on it?

To this challenge, many believers still objected. If the Shroud was truly the holy cloth that had wrapped Jesus' body, it would be blasphemy for mere humans to presume to put it through tests. It would be even

"This [the Gospel accounts] is the same evidence that the artist who created the Shroud used to make it look as realistic as possible."

Graduate student in geology,
Steven Schafersman,
Rice University

"One of the things that shook my natural predisposition to scepticism about the Turin shroud was precisely that it could not at all easily be harmonized with the New Testament. . . . No forger starting, as he inevitably would, from the details of the Gospels, and especially that of the fourth [John's], would have created the shroud we have."

Anglican Bishop
John A.T. Robinson

worse to lay hands on that precious blood. We would be like "doubting Thomas" in the Bible: He saw Jesus after the Resurrection and doubted that it was really the person whose death on the cross he had witnessed three days earlier with his own eyes. Only when he had touched Jesus' wounds would he believe. "Blessed are those who have not seen and yet believe," said Jesus. If we were to doubt and test the Shroud, wouldn't Jesus say the same to us?

So went the arguments of many pious Christians. Yet others knew that such tests would be the only way to prove conclusively the Shroud's authenticity.

Testing the Shroud for Blood

Finally in 1973, permission was granted to test the Shroud. This would be the very first time a scientist would lay hands on the precious "Shroud of Jesus." A team of specialists planned a small number of tests. Scientists would test the blood, the linen cloth itself, and surface particles removed from the cloth by sticky tape.

Were the Red Stains Really Blood?

In 1973 a blood expert named Dr. Giorgio Frache from the University of Modena, Italy, was given several threads from the "bloody" areas of the Shroud. He tested these threads with a chemical solution of benzidine. If the threads contained blood, the clear benzidine should have turned blue when it came near the bloodstained threads. The results were negative. Dr. Frache's benzidine did not turn blue.

Textile and Pollen Analysis: The Shroud Had Been in the Middle East

Although Dr. Frache's blood test had been negative, two other tests done at this time proved more positive. These tests seemed to favor the genuineness of the Shroud.

First, Dr. Gilbert Raes, a specialist in textiles (or fabrics) was consulted. By studying the Shroud fabric, Raes might be able to identify when and where the cloth was made. He was given some tiny samples of the Shroud cloth. Dr. Raes discovered something very curious: This cloth, which first appeared in France in 1355, had been made in the Middle East. This region includes Jerusalem and Bethlehem. It is the part of the world where Jesus lived and died. We also know it as the Holy Land.

The Shroud is made of linen, which comes from the flax plant. When Dr. Raes looked at the Shroud threads under his electron microscope (a special microscope that can magnify objects up to 100,000 times), he found traces of cotton which grew in the same area beside the flax plants. Dr. Raes counted about twenty twists in one inch of the cotton fibers from the Shroud. These twists identified it as Middle Eastern cotton. American plantation cotton is quite different in this respect. It has about sixty twists per inch of fiber. The number of twists could be clearly seen under the microscope. There could be no doubt that the Shroud's linen originated in the same surroundings where the cotton grew, which was definitely in the Middle East.

The last of the 1973 tests also pointed to the Middle East and, more precisely, to the Dead Sea. Dr. Max Frei was a detective. He was the chief of the criminology laboratory of the Zurich, Switzerland, police department. And he was an expert in identifying pollens.

All plants produce pollens. They are so small that they cannot be seen without the aid of a microscope. Pollens have a hard outer wall (the *exine*). Because of this shell, pollens can survive a long time after falling off their plants. One important fact about pollens is that each plant produces its own specific type of pollen, different from all others. An expert looking at pollens through a microscope can tell exactly what species of plant a pollen comes from. Another important fact is that pollens are found everywhere that dust gathers, such as in the corners of rooms and on

Map of the Middle East where Dr. Raes said the cloth was woven and from where Dr. Frei said pollens found on the Shroud came.

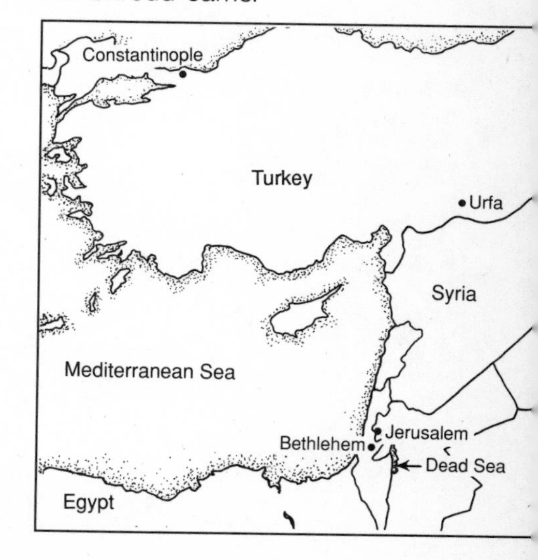

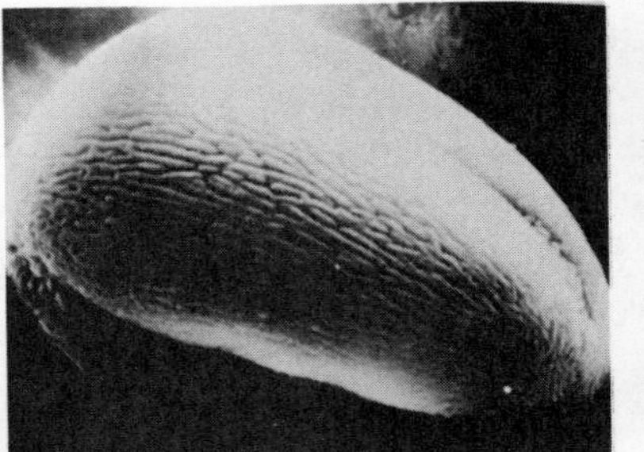

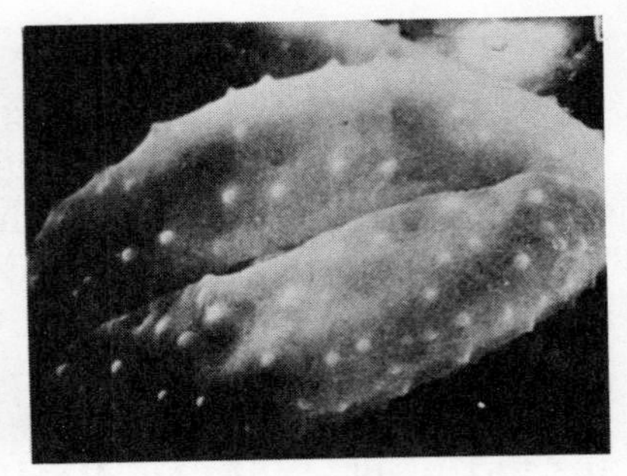

Magnified photos show three types of pollen which Dr. Max Frei found on the Shroud.

cloth. Dr. Frei knew that there must be pollen on the Shroud.

In 1973 Dr. Frei took pollens from the Shroud by pressing several sticky tapes against the Shroud material. Each tape was labeled, noting what part of the Shroud it had been pressed to. The pollens were then viewed by Dr. Frei through the large electron microscope in his lab.

Frei found pollens from fifty-six species of plants on his Shroud tapes. Only seventeen of these plants grow in France or Italy, where we know the Shroud has been since 1355. The other thirty-nine plants grow in the Middle East. This seems to be overwhelming proof that the Shroud has spent most of its history *outside* Europe, and most likely in the Jerusalem-Dead Sea area.

Frei also found pollen from three plants that grow in Southern Turkey, where the cities of Urfa and Constantinople are located. The reader should keep in mind this Urfa-Constantinople clue, for we will return to it later in this book.

Frei's most important discovery was that some of the pollens come from a species of plants called halophytes. Halophytes only grow in soil which is rich in salt, as is found around the Dead Sea. This sea is called "dead" because it is saturated with salt. Nothing can live in its waters. Naturally, the soil around its shores is salt-rich. Halophytes are thus rare and special plants, and their presence provides positive evidence for the Shroud's whereabouts before it came to Europe. All this agrees with Dr. Raes' findings that the Shroud was woven in the Middle East.

Does this pollen and textile information prove anything about the image of the man on the Shroud? No, it does not say anything about the image, only about the origin of the cloth. But if the Shroud *is* Jesus' burial wrapping, it *had* to come from the Holy Land. We now know that it does.

While these exciting tests seemed to be leaning toward the Shroud's authenticity, another man was seriously questioning it with theories of his own.

Nickell: An Artist Made the Shroud's Image

During the period 1973-1978, Joe Nickell first came out with his theory about how the image of the man on the Shroud was made. Mr. Nickell is a private detective and stage magician who has also worked in a museum. His occupation as detective familiarized him with crime-solving techniques (criminology). His job as a magician taught him how people can be fooled by clever tricks. His experience working in a museum made him familiar with art and artistic techniques such as would be used by a clever artist who wished to forge a shroud. Mr. Nickell brought all this experience into play in his attempt to prove that the Turin Shroud was a fake created by a cunning artist. He believes that he has solved the mystery of the Shroud.

Mr. Nickell is sure that the Shroud's image was formed by means of red colored powder, not liquid paint. The most probable powder was jeweler's rouge. This is a very fine, smooth powder used by jewelers to polish gold and silver. A form of jeweler's rouge was certainly available in the fourteenth century, when, according to Nickell, the Shroud was made.

In order to prove his theory, Nickell tried to form an image of a face on a cloth with jeweler's rouge in several different ways. His first attempts resembled the Shroud face but were unsatisfactory as proofs. They were too blurred and did not contain the fine details seen on the actual Shroud.

"Joe Nickell has produced negative images identical, for all practical purposes, to those on the shroud. His technique is embarrassingly simple."

Graduate student in geology, Steven Schafersman, Rice University

"Jackson has analyzed some of Nickell's images with the VP-8 system, but the results have been quite disappointing."

Thermal chemist Ray Rogers, Los Alamos National Scientific Laboratory, member of STURP

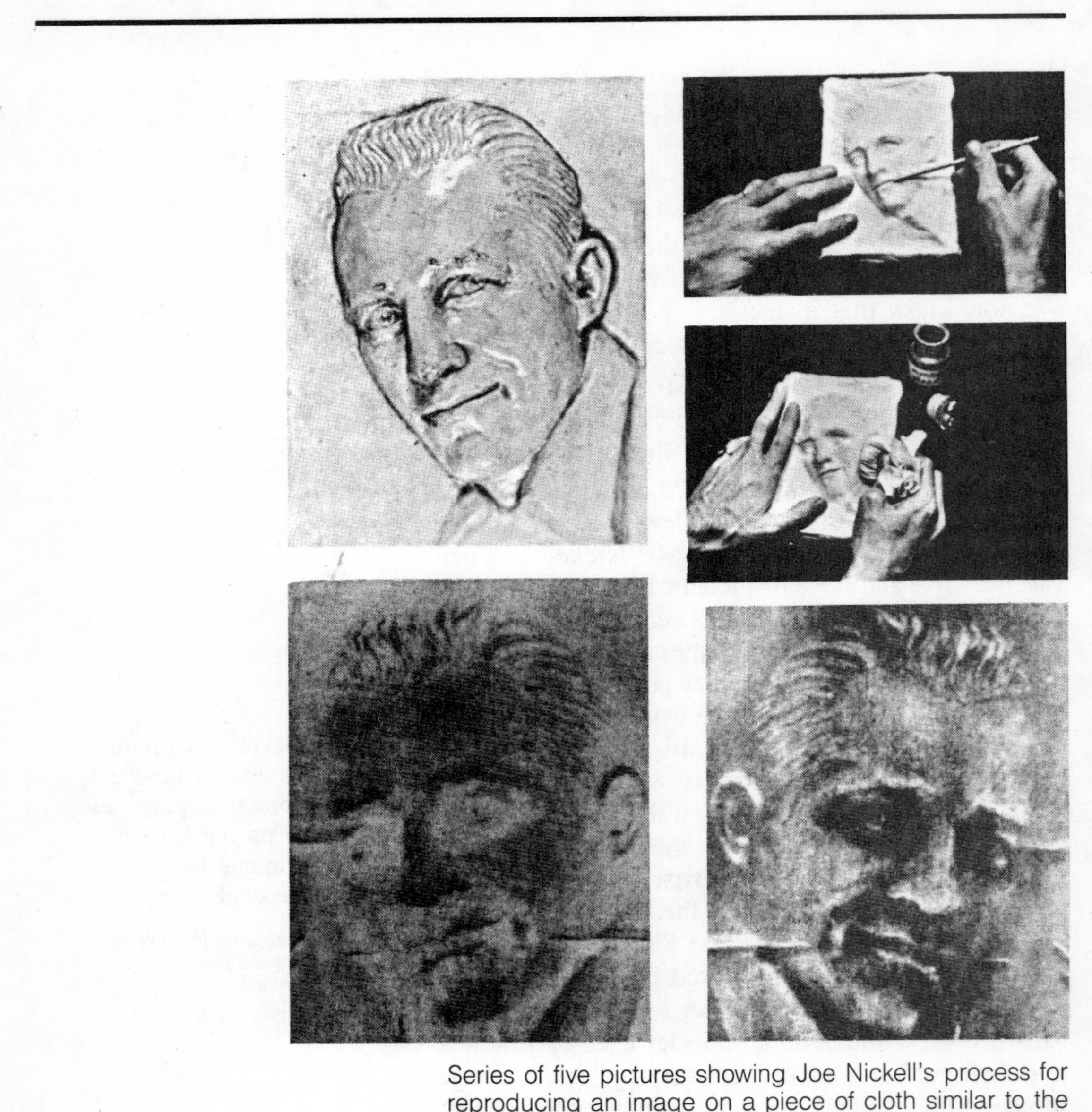

Series of five pictures showing Joe Nickell's process for reproducing an image on a piece of cloth similar to the image on the Shroud. Upper left: a suitable bas-relief is chosen. Upper right: wet cloth is molded to the relief and when dry, powdered pigment (myrrh and aloes) is rubbed on with a cloth-over-cotton dauber. On the bottom left is the image which results, as a positive, and on the bottom right as a negative.

Using another technique, he had better success in producing a face which was similar to that on the Shroud. He used a statue. He covered the face with a wet linen cloth similar to the linen Shroud. Then he pressed or molded it to the statue's face, using a pointed instrument to press the cloth into corners and fit the cloth to the details of the face, such as smile lines around the mouth. Then he dusted on his jeweler's rouge very lightly with a powder puff. When he had carefully removed the still damp cloth from the statue's face, he carefully flattened it. The result was a shroud-like face with many details which resembled the markings on the Turin Shroud.

Negative photo of a rubbing image done by Joe Nickell using iron oxide as the pigment.

Unfortunately, there is a flaw in Nickell's experiment. Although the blood on the Shroud has seeped right through the cloth, as a liquid should do, the human image on the Shroud is remarkable in that it is only on the surface fibers of the cloth. Nowhere does the image penetrate between the fibers to the back of the linen. But whenever Nickell's technique is tried on a linen cloth, the surface below is red with jeweler's rouge that has filtered through the cloth.

Nevertheless, Nickell is sure that his imitation and the alleged artist's confession of 1355 are proof that the Shroud of Turin is a fake.

If the image on the Shroud is in fact composed of jeweler's rouge, he may be correct. Jeweler's rouge is a form of iron oxide. (Iron oxide is what happens to old iron. Rust is a form of iron oxide.) If Nickell is right, there would have to be enough iron oxide on the Shroud to be seen by the naked eye (since the image can be seen). Scientific tests on the Shroud should show that iron oxide is the main ingredient on the image. Nickell's theory would thus be one of many that scientists would keep in mind when they did further tests on the Shroud.

Four

The STURP Team Is Chosen

In 1578 the Shroud first arrived in Turin, Italy. The year 1978 was thus the 400th anniversary of that event. The Archbishop of Turin decided to take the Shroud out of its vault and display it publicly. For about forty days in the summer of 1978 the Shroud, in a special glass-enclosed case, was shown to about three million people who came to Turin just to see it. On some days the lines reached back for blocks outside the Cathedral of St. John the Baptist. Many of these people believed the Shroud to be the actual cloth bought by Joseph of Arimathea to wrap Christ's body nearly 2000 years ago.

The display case made for this viewing was enormous. The entire Shroud could be seen behind the glass. The glass was polarized so that the bright floodlights which constantly bathed the Shroud and the camera flashes from millions of photographs would not fade or damage the image. The glass was also bulletproof. Inside the case, the atmosphere (temperature and moisture) was perfectly controlled for the safety of the precious cloth.

On this occasion, while the Shroud was removed from its vault, a team of American scientists received

Construction of a special nitrogen storage case to preserve the Shroud during the 1978 exhibition.

Three-dimensional photo of the Shroud front using the VP-8 image analyzer developed by NASA. This three dimensionality seems to prove that a real figure was once wrapped in the Shroud.

permission to study it with sophisticated scientific instruments. They were to be joined by scientists from Europe, such as Drs. Raes and Frei. This investigative team was called STURP, the Shroud of Turin Research Project. STURP would conduct non-destructive tests (that is, they could not harm the cloth or the image) to learn what was on or in the cloth. The testing would go on for five days and nights, 120 consecutive hours.

Who Are the Members of the STURP Team and Why Were They Chosen?

Why did the Shroud authorities choose STURP to push ahead with the scientific testing of their most sacred relic? The STURP team was accepted because of the results of some preliminary testing which they had done on photos of the Shroud in 1977. This work impressed Fr. Adam Otterbein and Fr. Peter Rinaldi (president and vice president of the Holy Shroud Guild in the U.S.) as an honest and unbiased quest for information.

The organizers of STURP were Drs. John Jackson and Eric Jumper. It was their idea in 1977 to do some tests using Enrie's 1931 black and white Shroud photos. They hoped to learn if the image on the Shroud could have been formed by contact with a human body. They found that in the Shroud's image there is encoded certain three-dimensional (3-D) information which a painter could not have put there. This information consists of shades of color which could only have come from a three-dimensional body. The following paragraphs describe how this important discovery was made.

3-D Testing

STURP's preliminary experiments were done with two recently invented devices: They are a microdensitometer and a VP-8 image analyzer. A few years before, these devices had helped the U.S. government make up a 3-D model of the surface of Mars by using black and white photos sent back by an orbiting spacecraft. Black and white pictures consist of white, black, and all shades of gray in between. The black parts are thick or dense with black color. The white portions have no black color in them. The grays are somewhere in between these extremes. The microdensitometer measures (*meter*) these amounts of black or density (*densito*). It measures every tiny (*micro*) difference in density. It gives each subtle shade of gray a number. For example, if black is ten and white is zero, charcoal gray might be nine, medium gray might be five, and so on.

These numbers are fed into the VP-8 image analyzer which converts the numbers to vertical relief or heights. The darker parts are the high points and the lighter parts are the low points. So, from the Mars photos, we now have a model of the hills and valleys on the surface of the planet Mars, though no one has ever set foot on the planet.

What is more, the VP-8 can project the 3-D model on a special television screen. Then the model can be turned in any direction so that we can see it from every side.

When these devices were used with Enrie's photos of the Shroud, a perfect 3-D model appeared on the screen. This could be turned sideways so that the Shroud man's face could be seen in profile. It was a perfectly formed 3-D man. This does not occur with artists' paintings, which result in distorted 3-D models. Thus, this seemed to be proof that the Shroud had once wrapped the body or a statue of a man and was not merely painted.

Would Nickell's Theory Produce a 3-D Image?

We must return, for a moment, to Joe Nickell's imitation of the Shroud. Recall that his theory used a statue of a man and dry colored powder rather than paint. Would it pass the 3-D test? It did not. Parts of the face which had too much colored powder jutted

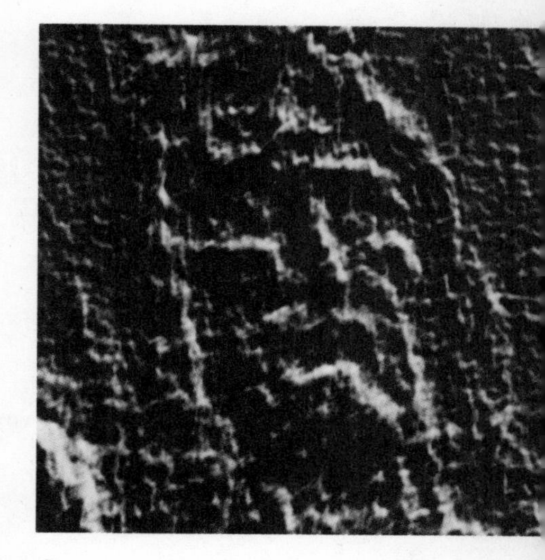

Closeup of three-dimensional face photograph.

"In summary, the historical, gospel, iconographic, pathological, physical, and chemical evidence against the cloth of Lirey seems overwhelming."

Author and detective Joe Nickell

"Somewhere along the way, you'd think a forger would have made some mistake, but there aren't any . . . . When you add up everything we know, the argument against a forgery acquired a certain force."

Member of STURP, John Jackson

out like mountain peaks. There was great distortion. Certainly, Nickell could keep repeating his experiment until he had just the right amounts of jeweler's rouge on his copy to produce a perfect 3-D face such as was on the Shroud. But how could the supposed original fourteenth century artist have got it so perfect without the aid of the two sophisticated twentieth century devices? Here was a serious flaw in Nickell's theory. The Shroud of Turin has perfect 3-D information in it. Nickell's image does not.

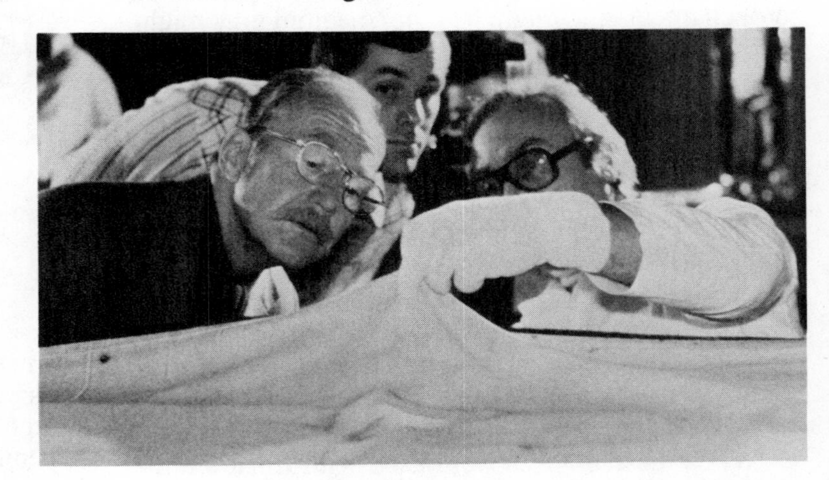

Ray Rogers, John Jackson, and Giovanni Riggi take the first look at the underside of the Shroud in 400 years. The Poor Clare nuns sewed a backing cloth on the Shroud centuries ago to help protect it.

Another of STURP's members had done research on paint ingredients. He was Dr. Ray Rogers, a thermal chemist from the Los Alamos Laboratory. Rogers is a specialist in what happens to substances when they have been heated. Since the Shroud had been in a fire in 1532 and thus had been subjected to great heat, Dr. Rogers would be able to analyze the substances on the cloth and how they might have been affected by the fire.

From his study of paint ingredients he knew that the colors in paints come from animals, plants, or minerals. The first two are called organic colors or pigments, since they came from living organisms (plants and animals). The third are called inorganic colors or pigments. He learned that under great heat all organic colors will run or change color. Inorganic colors such as red iron oxide (a mineral pigment from red soil) and the orange-red color vermilion (made from mercuric sulfide—an inorganic pigment—the source of the color in mercurochrome) turn black when heated.

Besides these facts, he learned that old and dried organic colors tend to run if water is added. Since the image of the Shroud man was doused with water at the time of the 1532 fire (recall the diamond-shaped water marks on the Shroud), these areas could be checked for signs of any running paint due to the dousing.

It stands to reason, Rogers argued, that if any of these paint pigments were on the image or the blood areas of the Shroud, they should either run, change color, or blacken on the parts of the Shroud nearest the burn holes (where the fire was the hottest on the cloth). The Shroud would have to be observed very carefully, even under a microscope, to see if there was any evidence for the presence of paints.

Dr. Rogers also researched the various liquids in which paint color can be mixed. A liquid of some sort is needed to "bind" the colored particles together into paint. By mixing in more liquid, the paint becomes thinner; by mixing only a small amount of liquid, the paint can be made thicker.

What sorts of liquids are used to make paint? What liquids were known to painters in the fourteenth century? How can science find out if these liquid binders are on the Shroud? These questions show how thoroughly STURP went about its testing. They left no stone (or particle) unturned.

Dr. Rogers' research turned up the answers. The liquid binders known to medieval painters were egg whites, egg yolks, animal fat, fish glue, plant gums (sap and resin), honey, and even ear wax. Sometimes linseed oil or walnut oil were also used in painting. The pure organic or inorganic color particles were

"A major stumbling block to the claims of authenticity has always been the fact that the 'blood' stains are unaccountably still red."

Author and detective Joe Nickell

"The blood appears too red, but this is explained naturally. When a person has been badly beaten, large amounts of bilirubin are formed."

Chemistry professor Dr. Alan Adler, Western Connecticut State University

Trucks arrive at the Royal Palace in Turin, Italy, bringing scientific equipment to test the Shroud.

stirred into one or more of these liquids or gels to make a paint which could be applied with a brush.

Luckily, all these mediums (liquid color-binders) have one thing in common which could be looked for by the scientists. All of them contain protein matter. (As we know, eggs are a good source of protein in our diets.)

So now STURP was equipped with solid information. They knew what to look for to determine if, in fact, the Shroud was a painted forgery. If they found any evidence of protein on the image, then the Shroud would likely be a fake. If they found evidence of colors running or of color changes near the burn marks, this too would mean the Shroud image was a painting.

Cooperation of Religion and Science

On October 8, 1978, the public showing of the Shroud came to an end and the testing began. The tests and their scheduling had been carefully planned. Some of the scientists slept while others worked. The American STURP team had flown tons of sophisticated equipment overseas to Turin for the tests. This equipment included a special table. On it, the Shroud could be spread out its entire length and held in place by magnets placed above and below.

Think for a moment about what was happening. Science had been invited by the Catholic Church to decide whether the Shroud, its most precious possession, was the real thing. Science was being invited to perform tests on blood that might be the actual blood of Jesus Christ, one of the world's greatest religious teachers. It was to be a cooperative effort between science and religion the likes of which had never occurred before: religion had never deliberately placed its faith in the hands of scientists. There had always been a sort of rivalry between them. What would the scientists do with this opportunity?

It is a scientist's duty to ask questions. All untested theories or claims should be doubted until they are proved true or false. There is still a great deal in

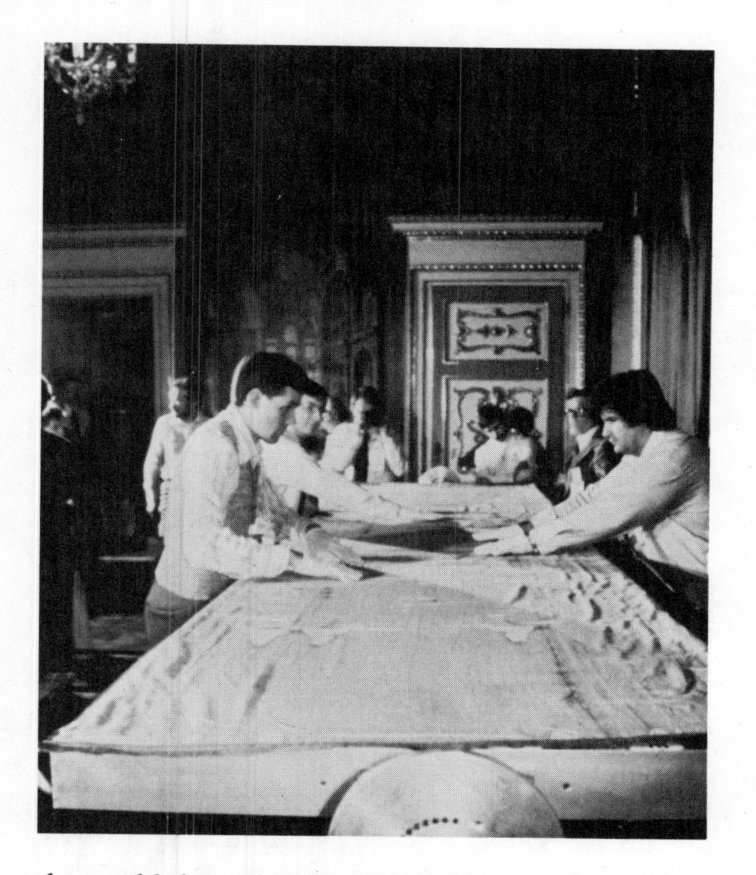

Members of STURP smooth the Shroud into position on the specially designed table which would hold it during the five days of testing.

the world that science does not understand. But the scientists were confident about their ability to solve the mystery of the Shroud. If there was paint or color pigment on it, they would soon find it. They were sure that they could penetrate the riddle of the faint image of the crucified man on the Shroud's surface. But as we will see in the next chapter, the mystery of the Shroud is not easily solved.

"The fact that STURP is composed entirely of religious believers makes it an extremely odd group of scientists indeed, and not one you would credibly consider predisposed to skeptical behaviour."

Graduate student in geology, Steven Schafersman, Rice University

"STURP is cast in the typical mold of most scientific American groups so far as their religious beliefs are concerned: a minuscule number of devout believers, a scattering of agnostics, with a majority of not particularly devout or convinced believers. You seem to be obsessed with the notion that scientists cannot be trusted unless they are agnostics. I can assure you that none of the believers among the STURP members went searching for the 'supernatural.' "

Vice president of the USA Holy Shroud Guild, Father Peter Rinaldi

Five

The Scientific Tests of 1978

STURP's work was monitored very carefully. First, the STURP team consisted of scientists from many leading laboratories and universities. Just to work at such places meant they were the best in their field. Second, the individual work of each member of STURP was checked for accuracy by the others in order to squelch any rumors that the group favored proving the Shroud was real. Third, they also cross-checked the results of the tests. If there were contradictory findings, they wanted to know why. Finally, the testing was as professional and "space-age" as it could be. The tests done and devices used sound like they come right out of *Star Wars.*

STURP Is Unable To Locate Frei's Pollens!

The testing did not go perfectly at first. In their efforts to be extremely precise in the removal of pollens to double-check Dr. Frei's work (who, it should be remembered, was the palynologist who tested for pollens on the cloth), STURP rigged up a tape applicator to press the tapes against the different points on the Shroud with uniform pressure. The STURP scientists were shocked when they examined the tapes for pollens and not one pollen was found

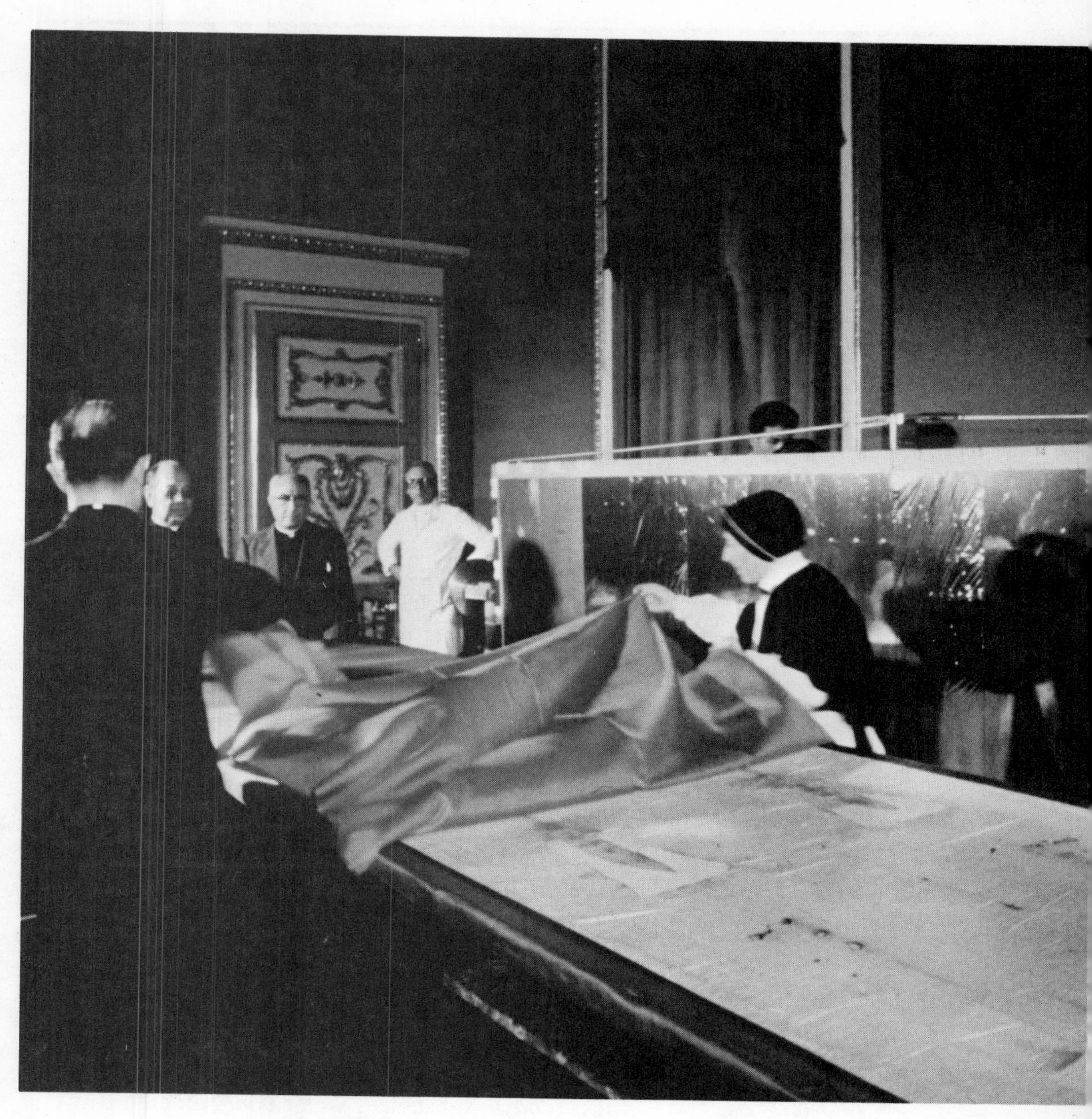

Monsignor Joseph Cottino, "Keeper of the Shroud," helps a Poor Clare nun remove the silk cloth which covers the Shroud in its jewelled box.

on any of them.

Immediately, Shroud opponents who learned of this began to hurl accusations at Dr. Frei. They even charged that he had planted the pollens on his tapes so they would conform to the supposed geographical travels of the Shroud from Jerusalem to France.

STURP was baffled. They were reluctant to believe that one of their team would be guilty of foul play. Yet it was true that there were no Shroud pollens on their tapes.

Then someone reread Dr. Frei's description of his procedure and noted that he had pressed his tapes to the Shroud by hand. With his thumb he had pressed the tape between the threads with a turning motion. In this way, his tapes had gained access to the deeper spaces below the surface of the Shroud where the pollens had settled. STURP now realized that their attempt to be precise and careful had almost caused the failure of the test.

Swiss criminologist Max Frei applies tape to the Shroud to obtain pollen samples for testing.

The next time the Shroud is removed from its vault for testing, the scientists plan to repeat Frei's work exactly as he did it. For now, Dr. Frei's pollen tapes are being accepted by STURP as accurate. They are being reexamined by other palynologists to confirm his identifications of pollens.

Further Tests: What Chemical Elements Are on the Shroud?

Another test STURP had decided to do was *reflectance spectroscopy.* By using this test, the scientists hoped to learn what chemical elements were present on the Shroud.

A chemical element is a substance which exists by itself in nature, unmixed with any other substance. It is a *basic* substance. Water is *not* an element; it is a combination of oxygen and hydrogen. Oxygen and hydrogen are elements. There are 103 elements in nature. All matter is composed of these elements.

Every chemical element can be identified by a certain combination, or spectrum, of color lines when viewed through a spectroscope. By scanning the entire Shroud cloth through the spectroscope, scientists can view the spectrums of every chemical on it. The team hoped that in this way they could learn what caused the image on the Shroud. They were particularly interested in searching for the color spectrum of iron oxide because it is the main component of red paint. The presence or absence of iron oxide would be a significant clue to the authenticity of the image on the Shroud.

One immediate result of this test was that the entire Shroud image showed the same spectrums (that is, the same elements were found all over the Shroud) except for the heels of the feet. What was peculiar about the heels, they wondered. By looking closely, they found that between the threads in the heel areas were particles of dirt. The particles were so small and so few that they could only be seen under a microscope. Since they were not visible to the naked eye, the dirt particles could not have been put there by an artist-forger in the Middle Ages. No one could have appreciated them before the invention of the microscope. And what could be more natural than dirt on the heel of a man who wore sandals?

Optical physicist Sam Pellicori is using a binocular microscope to examine the Shroud.

A surprising finding was that the image and the faint burn marks from the 1532 fire showed the same color spectrums. Could this mean that the entire image was a faint burn? If so, was science about to tell the world that a dead body could generate enough heat to burn its image in the surface of a linen cloth? Such a phenomenon does not happen in nature. It would be in the realm of a miracle. Was science about to deliver evidence for the Resurrection of Jesus?

One thing was certain from the examination done of the Shroud: The spectrum of the Shroud's image was significantly different from the known iron oxide spectrum. The image did not seem to be made of ordinary red earth pigment (red paint). This seemed to disprove the argument that the Shroud was a painting. But was it a scorch? Examination of the Shroud under ultraviolet light would reveal more about this question and whether or not the "blood" on the Shroud is real.

Is There Blood on the Shroud?

Some substances glow under ultraviolet (UV) light; for example, a white shirt glows purple under this light. These glowing substances are said to reflect this light. Other substances do not glow. They are said to *absorb* this light. Blood is one substance which absorbs UV light and does not glow. However, blood serum, the clear liquid in which blood cells are carried through the body, does fluoresce, or glow, yellow-green under the UV lamp.

When the UV light was flooded over the Shroud, the visible wounds went "black." But around these wounds were seen halos of fluorescence. What did this mean? One explanation could be that wherever there was blood on the Shroud there had to be blood serum. The serum would have penetrated into the linen even beyond where the red blood had stopped. Though the clear serum could not be seen, it was there. The UV light caused it to glow. Red paint would not have this result. Thus, it appeared that the bloody wounds were real. They must have transferred to the Shroud from a real bleeding body.

"These are scientists we're talking about . . . men who went . . . to prove that the Shroud was nothing more than a hoax—and they are coming away convinced that it is real."

Thermal chemist for STURP Ray Rogers, Los Alamos National Scientific Laboratory

But could the alleged fourteenth century artist have used real blood in his fake burial sheet? Here is where modern medical science comes in. Dr. William Bucklin of the Houston, Texas, Medical Examiner's Office is a pathologist. Pathologists are doctors whose specialty is identifying causes of death by examining corpses. Dr. Bucklin had long had an interest in the Shroud. He identified the blood flows on the Shroud as the natural bleeding of a human body.

"What had happened to due scientific caution? It seems the answer is that many of the STURP scientists had made up their minds before ever viewing the cloth."

Author and detective Joe Nickell

(We have noted that physicians of the fourteenth century knew very little about the interior parts of the human body. It was not until about 1600 that Sir William Harvey discovered the function of the heart in pumping the blood through the body. He first learned the difference between veins and arteries. Veins bring blood to the heart while arteries carry blood out to the body. Veins and arteries bleed differently. None of this was known by doctors—or by artists—in the fourteenth century.)

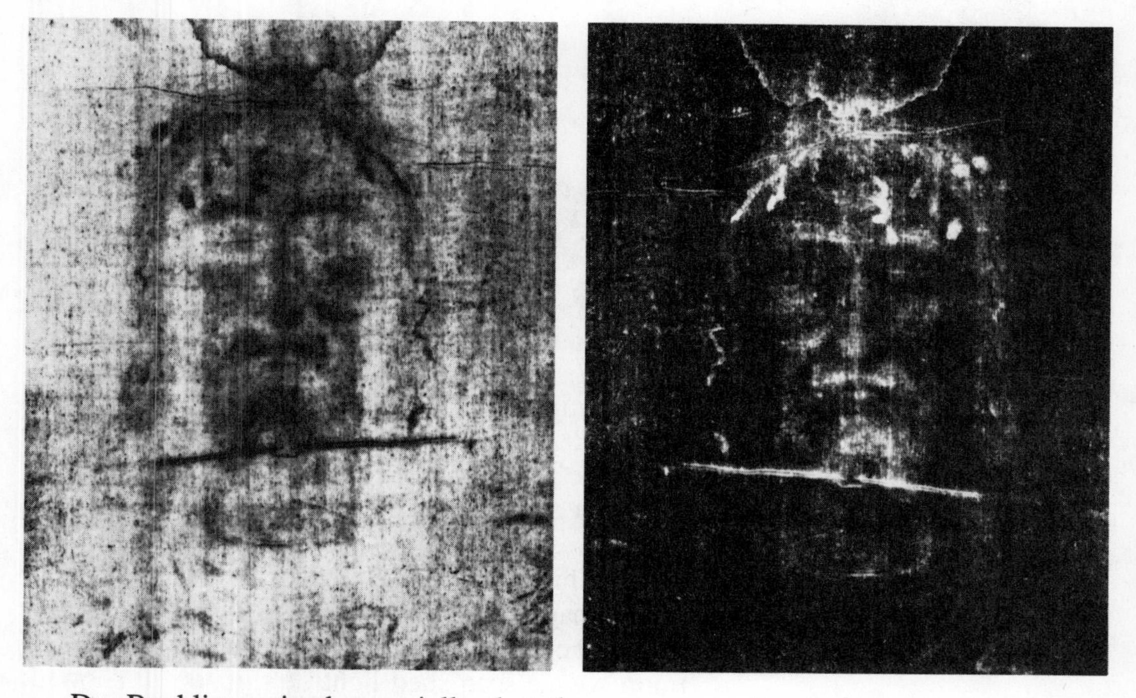

Vernon Miller's photographs showing the positive image (left) and the negative image (right) of the Shroud. Note the reverse "3" mark on the forehead.

Dr. Bucklin noticed especially that the reverse "figure 3" bloodstain in the middle of the forehead looked like bleeding from a vein (a "clean" seepage of blood), while the blood showing at the temple of the scalp appeared to be spurting blood as if it had bled from an artery. We do have veins and major arteries exactly in those locations on the scalp. Such natural-looking bloodstains were not likely to have been artificially put there by anyone from the fourteenth century. Dr. Bucklin said that this naturalness is true of all of the bloodstains on the Shroud. However, some pathologists do not agree with him. Most vocal has been Dr. Michael Baden, a medical

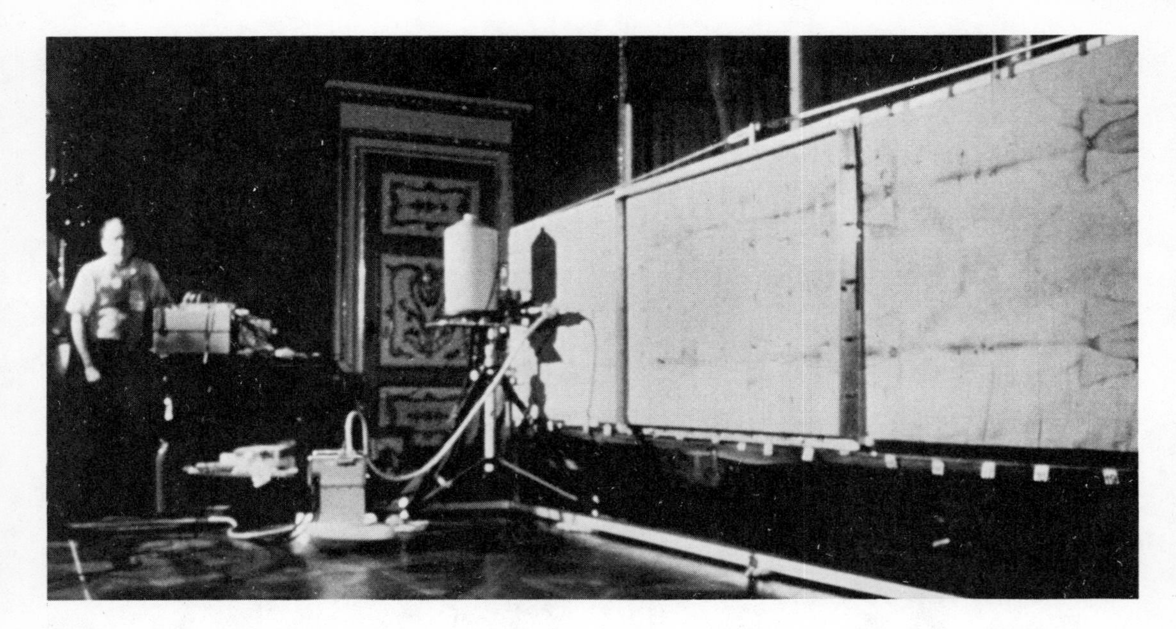

Scientists ready the equipment necessary to take x-ray pictures.

examiner in New York, who believes that blood would mat the hair and not flow outside the locks of hair as on the Shroud.

What about the body image itself? Recall that it closely resembled the markings known to be burn marks. This had led some religious scholars to wonder if the image could have been formed from heat or energy accompanying the Resurrection. The UV fluorescence scan shed light on this too. It showed: one, the image did not fluoresce; two, the burn marks from 1532 did fluoresce; and three, the burn marks that were on the Shroud before 1532 did not fluoresce. Scientists do not yet know why the image is similar to the pre-1532 burn marks, and they continue to look for further evidence of whether or not the Shroud image is a faint scorch.

Simple Low-Energy X-Rays: A Test for Iron

To shed further light on the blood controversy, STURP turned to simple, low-energy X-rays. We have all seen X-ray pictures. The principle is fairly simple. Hold a sheet of paper with typing on one side up to the light with the typed side away from you. The typing will appear against the light background. In a way, you have looked right through the paper as an X-ray machine does. Or place a metal BB pellet in the pocket of a white shirt and hold it up to the light. The BB will be seen. The density or solidity of the typing and of the BB block the light from passing through.

When the Shroud was X-rayed from end to end by the STURP team, the X-rays produced very bright pictures. The weave pattern showed up clearly. Individual threads could be seen.

Since iron is denser than linen cloth, if the image was made of a reddish paint containing iron, the iron should stand out and easily be seen on the X-rays. It did not. The image was almost invisible. Here was more evidence that the image was not composed of an iron-based paint: no image showed through in the X-rays.

However, at the edges or margins of the water stains (from the 1532 fire), high concentrations of iron oxide did show up. This fact should be remembered. STURP would remember it when Walter McCrone, the world's foremost particle specialist, declared in 1979 that the Shroud was without any doubt a painted forgery!

X-Ray Fluorescence: What Heavy Elements Are on the Shroud?

STURP performed another X-ray test in addition to the simple low-energy X-rays. This test is called X-ray fluorescence and it can detect substances other than iron such as iron oxide or mercury. These elements can be found in the types of paints used by artists in 1350. X-ray fluorescence showed only the barest trace of mercury. In addition, small amounts of calcium were found all over the Shroud. Most importantly, iron was detected *evenly distributed* over the entire linen cloth. This iron had not been visible in the simple X-rays of the Shroud.

Did the presence of iron mean the image had been painted? STURP's answer was "no." Approximately the same small amounts of iron were found to be on both the image areas *and* on the non-image, or clean, areas of the Shroud. Since that amount of iron was too small to be seen with the naked eye on the "clean" areas, the same "invisible" amounts of iron could not be producing the image. Therefore, they concluded, iron was not the cause of the reddish image.

The bloody areas contained much more iron. Since hemoglobin in blood is primarily iron, this test also supported the theory that a real bleeding body had once been wrapped in the Shroud.

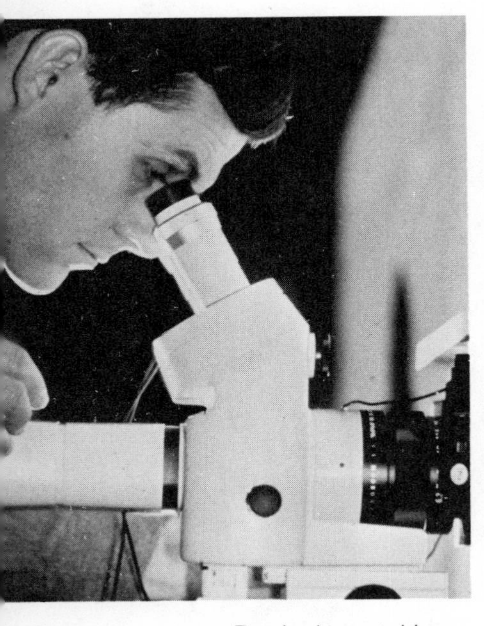

Dr. Jackson taking a microscopic photograph.

Simple Microscopy: A Most Revealing Test

In addition to the X-rays, STURP performed a simple, but ultimately more revealing test: looking at Shroud threads through the microscope at low magnification (magnified 30 to 40 times). The image appears reddish to the naked eye, but under magnification the fibers are straw-yellow in color. This came as a surprise to STURP scientists. However, they soon realized that it is a fairly normal visual fact. When color comics are seen up close, pink flesh tones are found to be collections of red dots, quite different from the way the color appears from a distance.

Also, under this magnification, one sees that the yellow fibers are only on the tops of threads and never on the insides, which are clean and white. The color is only two or three fibers deep! Where more of the fibers are colored yellow, the image is darker, as on the nose area. A darker image is *not* caused by a darker yellow coloring. It is caused by a larger number of the yellowed fibers.

No solid particles can be seen, even at 50x (magnified 50 times). If the image had been made by brushing dry colored powder over the cloth, there would be evidence of particles. But particles the size of powders seem to be absent from the Shroud. This seems yet another proof that the Shroud image was not made by colored powders—certainly not red ones.

Also, under the microscope, the fibers were not seen to be cemented together as they would be if they had been painted. Moreover, the paint would have seeped into the threads as any liquid does when spilled. This seeping is called *capillarity.* Remember that the yellow-colored fibers are never on the inside. There is thus no color seepage or capillarity on the Shroud image.

The absence of colored powder, of cementation of fibers, and of capillarity is evidence that the Shroud image was not made by ordinary painting with liquid paints. It was not made by rubbing or dusting with colored powder.

What Have We Learned So Far?

The forty or so members of STURP are in agreement about the above facts. Each member contributed special information. Each bit of information fit into the total picture like a piece of a jigsaw puzzle. Minor disagreements were studied until their reasons could be understood.

Yet the Shroud's mystery was not solved. STURP had learned what the Shroud was *not.* It was not a painting or a rubbing. They had learned from the Middle Eastern pollens on it that the cloth had been in Jesus' world before 1355. Dr. Raes in 1973 had shown that the Shroud had been woven in the Middle East. But he had not shown *when* it had been woven. Dr. Frei's pollens had not shown *how long* before 1355 the Shroud had been in the Holy Land. Science had not shown that the man on the Shroud was Jesus himself.

The "Blood" Is Tested More Thoroughly

There was still one substance on the Shroud which had to be investigated more thoroughly. STURP had learned what the deep red substance that looked like blood was *not.* It was not paint or jeweler's rouge. True, this "blood" is seen on the Shroud everywhere

"McCrone demonstrated that the image and 'blood' areas of the Shroud contain certain significant amounts of iron oxide pigment particles."

Graduate student in geology, Steven Schafersman, Rice University

"They did find iron oxide on the Shroud, but in such a minuscule amount that they are convinced the iron is from the blood and from sources other than paint a forger might have used. They are equally convinced that, were it possible to remove all the ferric oxide from the Cloth, the image would hardly be affected. Ferric oxide contributes only ten-percent to the overall image intensity, by no means sufficient to account for the image."

Vice president of the USA Holy Shroud Guild, Father Peter Rinaldi

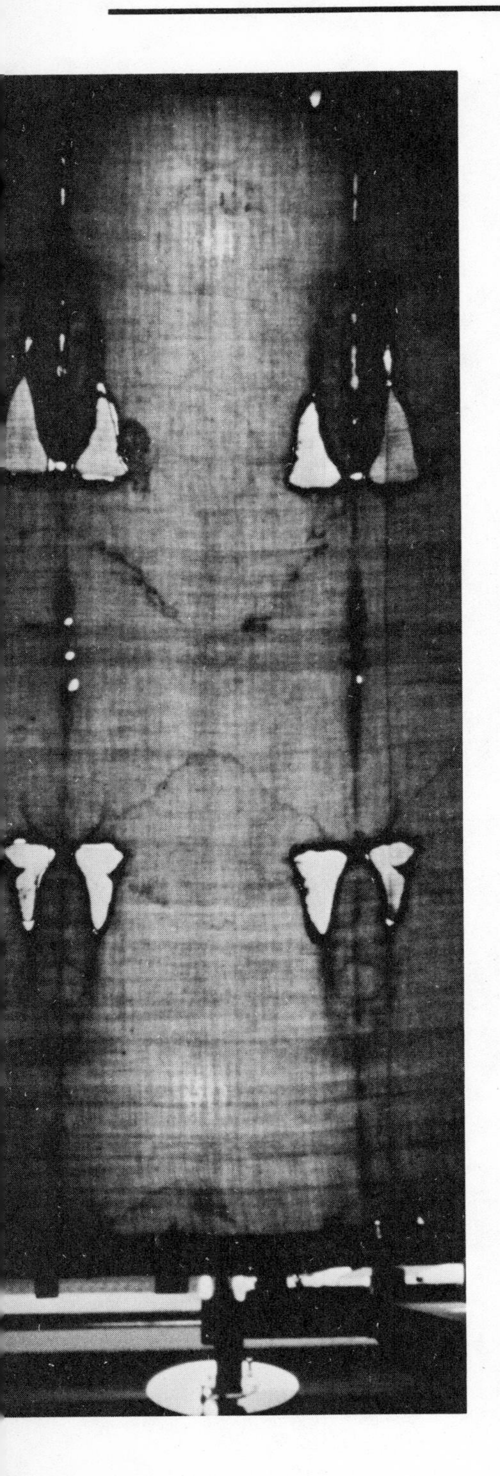

it should be, if the man of the Shroud was really Jesus. It is seen in the puncture marks on the scalp, in the numerous whip marks on the back, in the side, hands, and feet. However, many who have seen the Shroud have commented that the "blood" appears too red. Blood from a cut soon turns to brown when exposed to air.

The examination of the "blood" in 1973 had been a disappointment. It had not been proved that the red stains were truly human blood. The 1978 tests were more thorough. The "blood" was tested by all of the devices and techniques already mentioned which were used on the image. It seemed like real blood. But additional tests in well-equipped modern laboratories were also performed. These included blood-analysis tests commonly done by pathologists and chemical experiments designed to discover whether the blood-red threads were stained with real human blood.

This was another reason the sticky-tape samples mentioned earlier were taken. While the samples proved useless for identifying pollens, they did have enough fibers and particles stuck on them for these blood tests. Thirty-two samples were collected from different parts of the Shroud. Every part of the Shroud and every type of stain was represented among the samples. These included, for example, a non-image (clean) area sample, an image area sample, a blood area sample, and a side strip sample.

Walter McCrone Challenges the Shroud

Dr. Rogers sent these thirty-two tapes, each labeled to note the point on the Shroud which it touched, to Dr. Walter McCrone, world-famous microscopist (an expert on how substances appear under the microscope). It was thought that his skills could be extremely useful in identifying the cause of the image and especially the red particles on the tapes from the "blood" areas.

Dr. McCrone has his own laboratory, McCrone Associates, in Chicago, Illinois. He is the editor of

The Particle Atlas (1973), the authoritative three-volume book on the appearance of substances under the microscope. He achieved international fame by discovering that a famous, supposedly ancient, map of Vinland was a forgery.

The Vinland Map was thought to be a fourteenth century map proving that the Vikings had come to the North American continent about 150 years before Columbus. Yale University, which owned the map, invited Dr. McCrone to study it microscopically. Among the inks and pigments used to make this map, McCrone discovered titanium oxide which, he knew, was only developed as a synthetic black dye in the twentieth century. Therefore, he concluded the map could not have been drawn before the twentieth century and could not possibly have been made by Vikings. (Recent investigations have proven that Dr. McCrone may have been wrong about the Vinland Map. The inks used in the very first printed books by Johannes Gutenberg in the fifteenth century were found to contain titanium oxide in a natural form. This means that the ink used on the Vinland Map could indeed have derived from the fourteenth century. McCrone's conclusions are outdated by this new information.)

It was partially on the basis of his experience in working with historical objects that Dr. McCrone was invited to join STURP. No one considered it strange that Dr. McCrone initially expected that the Shroud did not go back to Jesus' time. Most of the STURP group had felt the same way in the beginning. As time went on, however, McCrone became increasingly convinced that the Shroud image was a fourteenth century painting. And in 1979, after working with Rogers' tapes, he shocked nearly everyone, including his colleagues in STURP, by announcing to the world his findings that the image was indeed, and without a doubt, just that: a work by an unknown artist in 1350.

What did McCrone find to put him so at odds with

Dr. Walter McCrone in his laboratory.

Opposite page: When the Shroud was backlit the image seemed to disappear. The patches covering the burned areas became lighter, but the possible blood flows on the forehead and down the arms were considerably darker. The water stains also were quite apparent.

all the scientific findings described so far? Let us allow him to speak for himself. The following statements are a summary from his first scientific report on the Shroud. It appeared in the magazine published by his own company, called *The Microscope,* Fall 1980.

> A blind study separated the 32 tapes microscopically into two groups: those with pigment on the fibers and those without. *None* of the control samples [those with no image] showed pigment particles whereas 18 body image and blood image areas showed significant amounts of pigment. . . . Many fibers in the image areas showed significant amounts of pigment. . . . Many fibers in the image areas appeared, in addition to the oxide particles, to be uniformly stained . . . yellow. To determine whether these fibers are also associated with the image we examined more than 8,000 fibers from both image and non-image areas. . . . The image areas had more stained fibers . . . than the non-image. . . . This shows that the image is made up of two components: an iron oxide pigment . . . and a uniform yellow coloring.

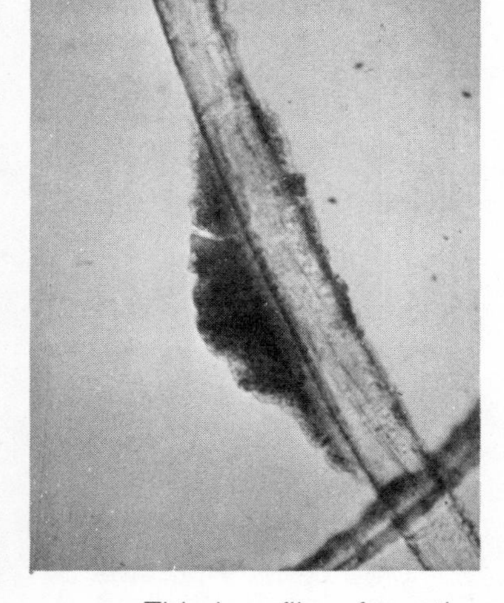

This is a fiber from the Shroud which Dr. McCrone stained with amido black.

After this first article, McCrone did analyze his particles chemically in order to verify the pigments he states were used to paint or enhance (darken) the image. He realized, too, that if pigment was to be proved, then also a liquid binder for the paint ought to be present—and also proved chemically.

Sure enough, in the microscope, he saw clusters of red particles bound together somehow. Would chemistry confirm this suggestion of liquid paint? McCrone used the same tests as those used by art conservators to identify paint mediums. The following quotations are from Dr. McCrone's second article (*The Microscope,* December 1980):

> There are numerous pigment particle aggregates [clusters] that behave as though held together by an organic binder. . . . Fibers from image areas were tested . . . with amido black. . . . Blue staining [was] observed, thus confirming the presence of a tempera paint. Colorless fibers from image areas and

> all control area fibers stain only slightly or not at all. . . . One must conclude that an artist has, at least, enhanced what would have been a far fainter original [authentic] image or he has produced the entire image. The date the artist did his work is therefore in the middle of the fourteenth century or earlier.

Dr. McCrone used amido black as a test for protein. There is protein in all of the known organic paint binders. Protein on the *image* would seem to indicate the presence of paint.

Dr. McCrone performed an important service when he collected and quoted several passages from various books on early painting. These quotations describe the practice of painting in a thin or diluted solution of watercolors on cloth. According to the authors of these books, cloth paintings very similar to the Shroud image were quite well known in the fourteenth and fifteenth centuries. Here McCrone seemed to find evidence that the Shroud was not one-of-a-kind. On the other hand, no painting on cloth from that period was done in the same monochrome (single color) tint as the Shroud image. None was as lifelike and anatomically accurate as the man on the Shroud. Unlike the Shroud, they look like ordinary paintings. The style of painting in the fourteenth century was not nearly so realistic as the Shroud figure, and the human form was almost never shown unclothed.

In a third published article (*The Microscope,* March 1981), McCrone claimed the presence of vermilion on the Shroud. Orange-red vermilion was used in early paintings to soften the flesh tones of the skin. By the time of this article, Dr. McCrone had sent all but one of the 32 tapes back to Dr. Rogers. This one tape supposedly contained "blood" from the side-wound of the Shroud man. It was here that McCrone found his vermilion.

The first newspaper announcement of McCrone's belief that the Shroud was a fake angered the scientists of STURP. Their own findings (as seen earlier)

"When, with 100 percent certainty, we [Alan Adler and John Heller] make a categorical statement that blood is present, believe it!"

Former Professor of Internal Medicine and Medical Physics John Heller, Yale University

"[Adler and Heller] are wrong. I know blood when I see it through a microscope, and there was no blood."

Director of the McCrone Research Institute, Walter McCrone

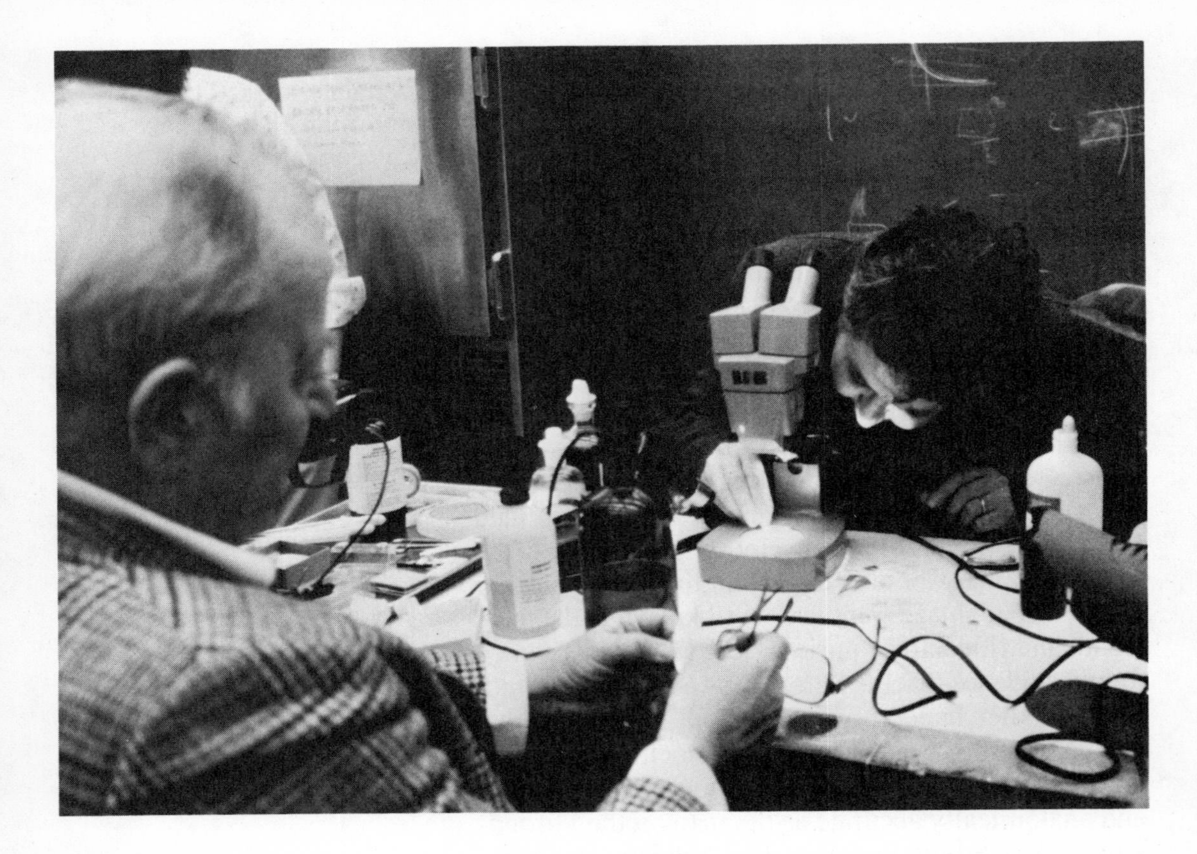

Drs. John Heller and Alan Adler performing microscopic studies to detect the presence of blood on the Shroud.

were tending to prove the authenticity of the Shroud. But they had agreed not to publish their articles until all their findings could be discussed and they could be absolutely certain about their statements. So far, their findings were opposed to McCrone's.

No one could explain how scientists examining the same object could "see" different things on it and arrive at totally opposite conclusions. Because of this disagreement the Shroud remains almost as much a mystery as ever.

Adler and Heller: The "Blood" is Blood

But in 1981 all hoped that further study of those 32 tapes might solve the mystery. If McCrone's studies could be proved correct, then the Shroud would have to be admitted as a forgery. The key would lie in the work of Dr. John Heller and Dr. Alan Adler. It was they who next received the tapes and who would examine them in ways McCrone had not thought necessary. McCrone had looked at the contents of the tapes under his trusted microscope. He had performed a single chemical test (amido black).

Drs. Heller and Adler would do a thorough chemical and microscopic analysis of the fibers on the tapes. They would see if blood was present; they would see if the image and the bloodstains were made of different thicknesses of red paint.

Their results were totally at odds with McCrone's. The story of their work reads like an engrossing whodunnit, full of unexpected twists and turns and surprising discoveries. Sherlock Holmes could not have done more than they did with the tapes.

According to McCrone, both image and blood were painted with red iron oxide and a protein binder (tempera paint). Adler and Heller (as did other members of STURP) found several different kinds of red iron particles.

The first type of red particle was described as *birefringent iron.* This is the iron oxide which the STURP tests found evenly distributed all over the Shroud. It is present in equal amounts on the image and on non-image areas. Since the amount of this iron is so small that it cannot be seen on the non-image area (the clean background of the Shroud), the same amount on the image area is not what the eye sees as an image. This finding was in total disagreement with McCrone who found *no iron at all* on the clean background, some on the image, and lots in the "blood" areas.

A second type of iron on the Shroud was of the non-birefringent type. This is a term which means the iron can be of the type found in blood or hemoglobin. Adler found this kind of iron only in the "blood" areas.

Finally, they found birefringent iron oxide parti-

"In view of the many tests conducted by Heller and Adler that did prove positive, I am prepared to accept these stains for what they purport to be—human blood."

Shroud researcher
Father Robert Wild

"The presence of blood cannot be 'considered as firmly established.' Not a single one of the chemical tests of Heller and Adler confirms the presence of blood."

Graduate student in geology,
Steven Schafersman,
Rice University

cles (meaning rust or possibly red earth pigment) actually embedded in linen fibers. Under magnification, these look like hollow bamboo stalks with iron "cannonballs" caught within the tube. This iron oxide was only found in the edges of the water stains from the fire of 1532.

Why Was Iron Inside the Cloth?

How, wondered Adler and Heller, could tiny red particles of iron oxide get *inside* the linen fibers? When an artist puts color on a cloth, the particles of color are applied to the *surfaces* of the fibers. So this red iron oxide was *not* paint. They concluded that the answer to the riddle of the red "cannonballs" inside the fibers had to do with two things: 1) the way linen cloth used to be made and 2) the fire of 1532.

1) In order to make flax into linen cloth, the flax used to be soaked in a natural body of water, usually a stream or lake, for a long time. This is called "fermenting" or "retting" the flax. During retting, two minerals, calcium and iron, are attracted to the cellulose (basic material) of the flax. Retting thus explains why the STURP X-rays, described in chapter four, showed calcium and iron scattered evenly all over the Shroud linen.

2) During the fire of 1532 water was poured on the very hot Shroud. Some of the iron which was attached to the flax migrated to the edges of the water stains as iron oxide. In this process the red iron oxide particles were "soaked" into the cloth and appear under the microscope as "cannonballs" embedded inside the fibers.

McCrone had not noted, as Adler and Heller did, that the tapes in question happened to come from a spot on the Shroud where a water stain appeared upon the body image. Only the detective work of Adler, who studied the ancient techniques of making linen cloth, helped to solve this riddle of the "cannonballs." He had read about the natural attraction of iron and flax atoms during the retting process. It might have been the high concentration of iron oxide in the water-stain margin that McCrone had misread as red iron-based paint on the image.

Trying To Remove the Image

Now Heller and Adler addressed themselves to the body imprint. Recall that the fibers of the Shroud image appear reddish to the naked eye but are actually yellow when viewed under a microscope. As Heller and Adler wrote, "All known organic dyes and/or stains, both natural and synthetic . . . can be extracted [removed] by some solvent." So they applied various solvents, some weak, some very strong, to the yellow fibers of the imprint. They found, to their surprise, that the color was not changed and not removed by these solvents. Only the strongest bleaches whitened the yellow body-image. This fact seemed to exclude the presence of paint.

Proving whether it was real blood on the Shroud was a fascinating bit of sleuthing by Heller and Adler. McCrone, you will recall, sought and found his protein binding material by applying a substance called

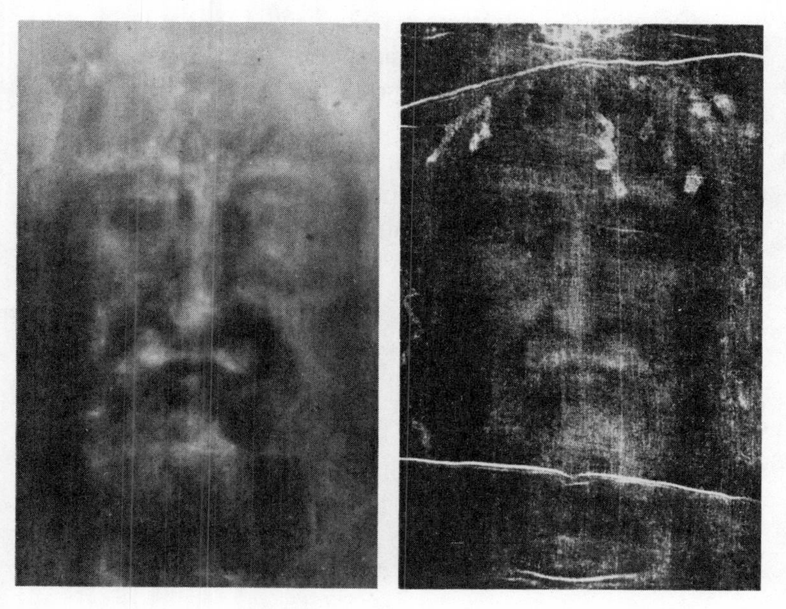

The picture on the left is a negative of a shroud image painted by the late Walter Sanford, a Chicago artist. The image on the right is the Turin Shroud.

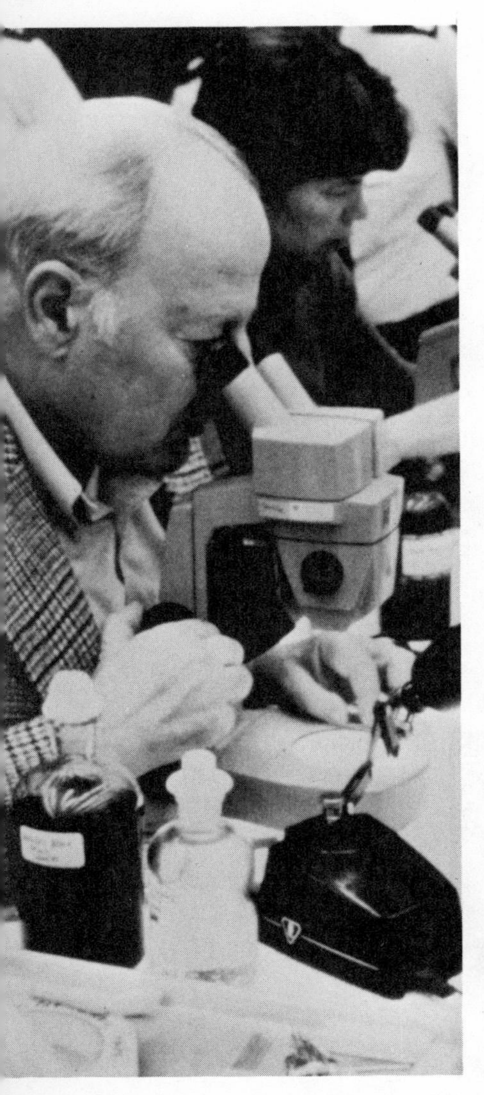

Dr. Heller attests that the "blood" stains on the Shroud are human blood.

amido black to the fibers on the Shroud tapes. They turned a blue color, proving, he argued, the presence of animal or vegetable protein in liquid form to bond the red pigment particles together as paint.

McCrone's conclusions were refuted when Heller and Adler discovered that amido black also stains ordinary cellulose (the chief component of linen) the same blue color. Furthermore, amido black worked even better on linen which once had been heated or scorched. In other words, amido black would stain the entire linen Shroud blue and is not a *specific* test for detecting protein.

The two STURP scientists found another test "specific for protein": *fluorescamine,* which makes even the tiniest traces of protein glow green under ultraviolet light. They found that all the red and orange "globs" (groups of particles) on the "blood" tapes glowed green. But "the fluorescamine tests were definitely negative on all fibrils away from blood areas." The iron found in the water-stain edges and the yellow body image fibers showed no trace of protein by the fluorescamine tests. Thus they are not associated with protein paint binders. Protein, a component of blood, was found only on blood-area tapes.

The blood fibers also tested positive for albumin, another component of real blood. Albumin was found only in blood fibers and in fibers immediately next to blood fibers. As mentioned earlier, all around the bloodstains on the Shroud would be the natural serum in which the blood cells flow through the body. When the blood dries, it retracts or shrinks back somewhat, leaving an invisible ring or halo of serum around the bloodstain. So it is with the Shroud. This serum, then, also tested positive for albumin.

Next, Adler and Heller tested the "blood" for the substances which give it its red color. These too were positively identified in the "blood" fibers. The high percentage of *bilirubin* (red blood-bile) that results from blood clotting is apparently the reason the

Shroud blood is so red. As mentioned earlier, this redness can still be noticed in the color photographs of the Shroud. The Shroud's blood must thus be clotted blood.

Shroud Blood Is Human or Ape Blood

Finally, the two blood specialists performed a test to determine if the blood was human blood. Antibodies in animal blood will attack human blood-albumin, but will not attack animal blood-albumin. And this is exactly what happened in the test. Pig, cattle, and horse blood were not attacked by animal antibodies, but the Shroud blood was. Adler and Heller concluded that the Shroud blood is definitely human or primate (large ape) blood (which, they caution, can sometimes react like human blood). But, as Adler remarked, "That is certainly not an ape on the Shroud."

When these findings are combined with the findings from observing the Shroud under UV light, the evidence seems very strong that the "blood" is real blood and not red ochre earth pigment plus vermilion, as Dr. McCrone argued.

A further argument against McCrone's theory is that the traces of eleven other elements that he found are all elements which are found in whole blood. However, he did *not* report finding any manganese, cobalt, or nickel—three impurities which are always found in red iron earth pigment. If the Shroud had been painted, the pigment would have to be an extremely pure form of iron oxide which would have been virtually impossible for a medieval artist to distill, and virtually unknown in art history.

But McCrone had another argument. Besides red ochre and vermilion, he had spotted some particles of other colors on the Shroud. This convinced him more than ever that the Shroud had been painted, since splashes or sprays of color can result from the mere presence of a cloth in an artist's studio.

Of course, this is not necessarily the case. It is commonly known that the Shroud's image was copied

"The work of Drs. Alan D. Adler and John H. Heller, chemical engineers in Connecticut, leads them to conclude that the blood traces in the Shroud are of mammalian, primate, and *probably* of human, blood."

Religious writer Frank C. Tribbe, *Portrait of Jesus?*

"The nature of the iron oxide on the Shroud turned out be very similar to an artist's pigment."

Director of McCrone Research Institute, Walter McCrone

This ancient rolling-stone tomb is said to belong to the family of Herod the Great, in the time of Jesus. Could a limestone tomb like this have had an effect on a burial cloth like the Shroud?

dozens of times by artists after 1355. Such tiny amounts of color could have gotten on the Shroud on those occasions. Also it is recorded that many of these copies were placed directly upon the Shroud as if to validate them or make them more authentic. (In the same way, a book autographed by the author has more value than the book alone.) Besides, STURP has argued, the scant amounts of artist colors on the Shroud are hardly enough to produce or explain the body's imprint. Traces of colors do not prove the Shroud to be an artist's hoax.

What Has Science Learned About the Shroud Image?

STURP did chemical, microscopic, and physical examinations of the Shroud, its fibers, and foreign particles on it. Having thus proved the various "applied pigment" theories false, the STURP team agreed that the imprint on the Turin Shroud is not composed of foreign material, is in the cloth itself, and is, in fact, caused by a fairly normal process.

As is well known, when linen cloth or paper is

left untended for a period of time, it begins to yellow. This yellowing is simply an oxidation or aging of the plant cellulose in the linen. Good examples of this oxidation or aging are the yellowing of old newspapers or the browning of a cut apple. The Shroud is yellowed with age, as we expect with old linen. The body imprint, STURP asserts, is an advanced stage of this process. Something on the cloth, whether sweat or body oil, has sped up the normal process wherever the body was close to or touching the cloth. STURP scientists calculated that contact of a body with a linen cloth for 24 to 36 hours is enough to speed up the yellowing.

Thirty-six hours, in fact, is the longest period the body could have been in contact with the Shroud. Beyond that time the bacteria which cause a corpse to decompose would contaminate cloth and, in time, destroy it. STURP found no evidence of decomposition on the Shroud. Indeed, the fact that the Shroud still exists is evidence that the body was not wrapped in its Shroud longer than 36 hours.

In 1942 a similar image-formation theory had been published by Dr. Jean Volckringer in Paris. He noted that when plants are pressed between the pages of books for several years, they leave very detailed sepia-colored imprints on the pages. These imprints are similar to the Shroud's imprint. They seem to be the result of an accelerated aging or degeneration of plant cellulose, the same process that occurs (but more slowly) in the normal aging of paper or linen.

Recently, archaeologists in Palestine have offered a new possible explanation of the image on the Shroud. They made further chemical tests of the Shroud sticky tapes and found traces of limestone. This Shroud limestone perfectly matches the limestone samples taken from burial chambers in Jerusalem that are similar to the one in which Jesus was buried. Experiments showed that this limestone will cause the surface of linen fibers to turn to the exact yellow color as on the Shroud. This process is sped up by heat, such as the heat imparted by a body—even a dead one. Here is a theory worth keeping in mind, though it too has its opponents.

STURP has said, and continues to say, that science has not figured out *yet* what caused the Shroud to yellow where the body touched it. The scientists of STURP believe they have learned—and proved—that the Shroud of Turin did once wrap a human corpse. They have also learned that the image was formed by contact and by closeness of the body to the cloth. However, they recognize that vapors or heat from a body will diffuse (spread out). Vapors will not perfectly imprint the details that we see in the Shroud's image. Only laser beams travel in straight lines through space. But how lasers could cause an image on an ancient shroud, they do not know.

Is this just a way of saying that the portrait on the

Drs. Jackson (middle) and Jumper (right) use a volunteer and a copy of the Shroud to test several theories, including whether or not the Shroud covered a real body.

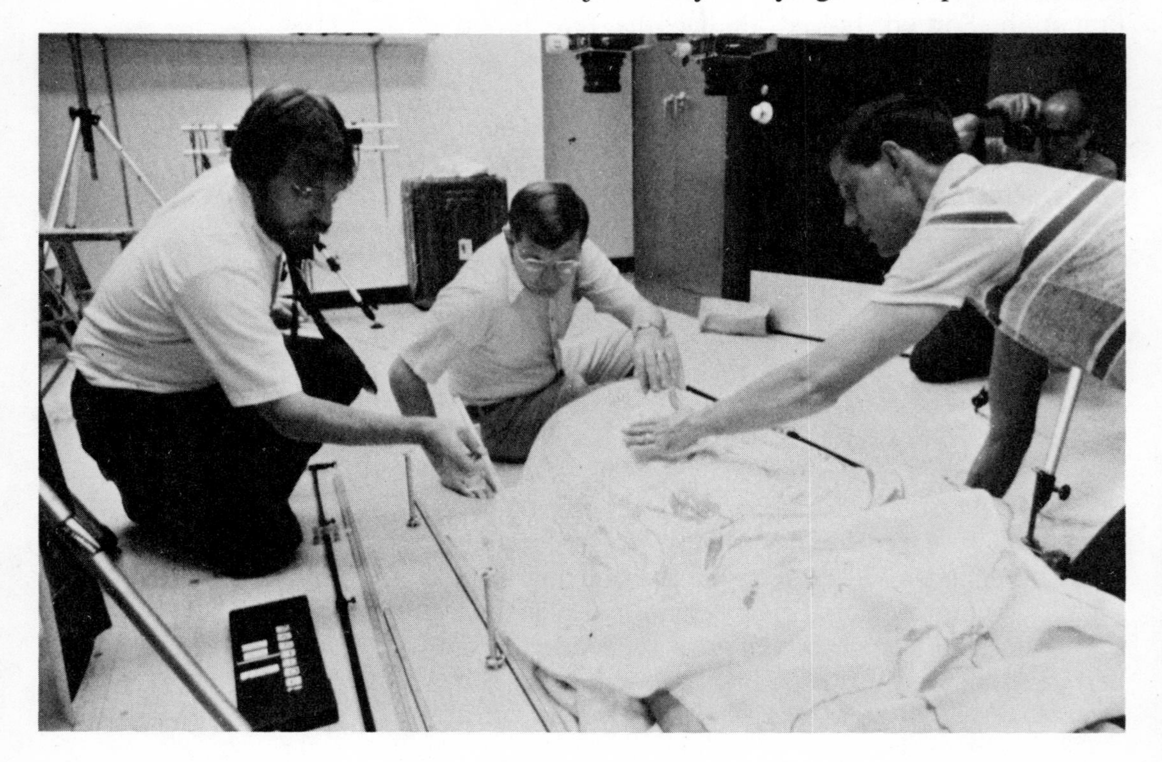

Shroud is a miracle? STURP has been accused by Joe Nickell and others of making this claim. STURP members strenuously insist that they are referring to a natural process and are not implying that the image was caused by a miracle.

It is one of the mysteries of the Shroud that Dr. Walter McCrone and STURP arrived at opposite conclusions from studying the same data. The puzzle of the Shroud will go on until someone clears up the dispute between McCrone and STURP: He sees iron oxide only on the image and blood areas, and none on the non-image areas; STURP sees it scattered evenly over the whole cloth, image and non-image alike.

The scientists who performed the tests described in this chapter all attempted to discover how the image on the Shroud of Turin was made and what it was made of. As for who the person of the Shroud is, this may be a task for historians to discover. And it is to the Shroud's early history that we now turn.

Six

The History of the Shroud: The Hidden Centuries

We have very few historical references to the Shroud before the letter of Bishop d'Arcis. This means from the burial of Jesus up to 1389—about 1350 years of nearly total silence. Can such a significant object go largely unnoticed, or at least unmentioned, for 1350 years? Were there at one time more records which have since been lost or destroyed? This is the stuff that mysteries are made of. Let us see what history can teach us about the Shroud.

The Shroud Is Mentioned in the Bible

Jesus' burial wrapping is a part of the Easter story of the Bible. All four Gospel accounts (Matthew, Mark, Luke, and John) tell how Joseph of Arimathea, a devoted follower of Jesus, bought a fine new linen burial sheet for Jesus' body after he was taken down from the cross. Is this sheet the Shroud which is today in Turin, Italy? A passage in the Gospel of John is probably the last "official," that is, Biblical, reference to this cloth. In John 20:19-36 we read that John and Peter ran to the tomb on Easter Sunday morning. Inside John saw the burial sheet, and he saw the *sudarium* or chin-band (for holding the jaws closed) rolled up in its own place. After this the record is silent.

This painting by sixteenth century artist Giovanni Battista della Rovere illustrates how a body would have been wrapped for burial in order to leave the head-to-head image we now see.

What the Gospel narratives do *not* say is equally important—and has, in fact, set in motion the mystery that has surrounded the Shroud of Jesus ever since: none of the Gospel writers say that the Shroud was saved after the events of Easter Sunday morning. John's last reference leaves it in the sepulcher. Also, the Gospel accounts do not mention an image on Jesus' burial sheet.

These omissions are one reason Bishop d'Arcis believed the Lirey Shroud could not possibly be the one referred to in the Bible. Wouldn't the Gospel writers have said something about preserving Jesus' burial linen with his precious blood on it? Wouldn't they have mentioned if it had contained a portrait of Jesus himself? As Bishop d'Arcis argued, this would seem to be proof that the Lirey Shroud with its image was not the same as the shroud of the Gospel accounts.

One explanation may be that the image was not yet visible on the cloth. Perhaps it only darkened little by little. (Remember what was said about the slow yellowing of linen.) If an image could not yet be seen on Easter morning, then the Evangelists (Gospel writers) could not mention one.

As to whether the disciples of Jesus did remove the burial wrappings from the tomb, the Gospels are indeed silent. There is evidence, described later, that they did take the Shroud. This evidence suggests they took it with them into hiding, for, as we read in the Bible, they feared for their lives. They would have known that if they "advertised" their valuable possession, it might become a target for either Romans or Jewish zealots.

Those who were responsible for Jesus' crucifixion seemed determined to stamp out the new—Christian—sect. The Easter story shows that they would do anything to erase the memory of Jesus. They would seize and destroy the Shroud if their attention was drawn to its survival. So the Shroud was kept hidden, and the Gospel stories are silent about its removal from the tomb. The Bible is silent on many other things as well. For instance, details about much of the first thirty years of Jesus' life are omitted.

Details of the Crucifixion Found in the Gospels

Before we leave the Gospel accounts, let us recall some other details of the story. The way in which these details compare with information gleaned from the Shroud itself gives us strong historical evidence for the genuineness of the Shroud.

We read that Jesus was crowned with thorns. The Roman soldiers mocked him with the "crown" for pretending, as they thought, to be King of the Jews. Artists always depict this as a wreath, and Matthew and Mark do say that the soldiers "twisted together" a thorny crown. But look at the puncture wounds on the scalp of the Shroud man. They cover his whole head, not as a Roman victory wreath would, only around the forehead, but as a clump of thorns would if pressed into the scalp. Such thorny "tumbleweeds" must have been a familiar sight to Romans and used as kindling for their guard fires. Some arranging or

These photos of the Shroud man's head and shoulders show how the crown of thorns would have punctured most of his scalp, causing it to bleed. Notice also what appears to be a single long lock of hair, thought by some to be worn by Jewish men of the time.

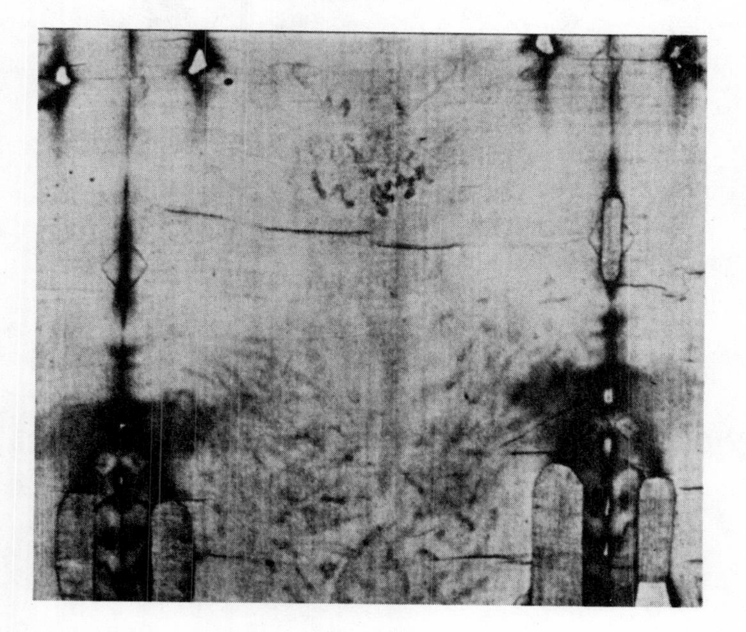

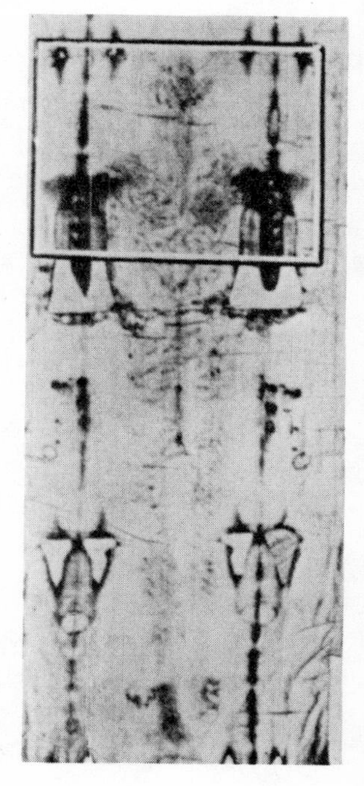

twisting would be necessary, but it does not seem probable, when one thinks about it, that a soldier would take the time and effort, as well as the pain of pricked fingers, to carefully lace together a wreath of thorns, when a "tumbleweed" was so available. And the larger and more grotesque the "crown," the greater would be their joke, and their laughter. Thus from the Shroud we picture a crown of thorns which is different from those depicted by artists, but apparently more accurate.

Let us not forget the real importance of the crown of thorns in judging whether the Turin Shroud shows Jesus' portrait. The Romans mocked Jesus as a "king" with a crown of thorns. There could not have been many other "kings" who were crucified and who would have been similarly mocked. Of the thousands of victims of Roman crucifixion, the man of the Shroud ranks among a very small number who might have left this imprint on a burial cloth. This certainly

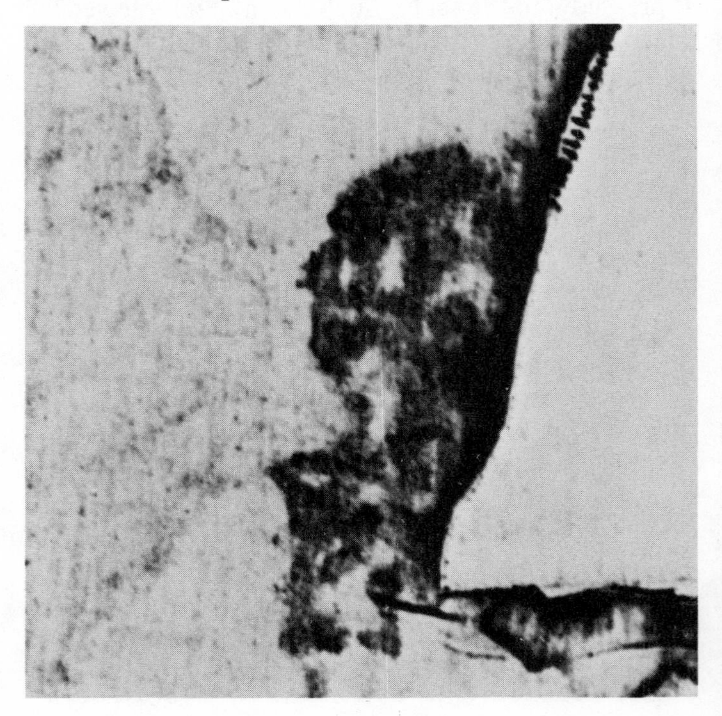

This closeup of the side wound shows a patch covering part of the "blood" flow.

improves the chances that he really is Jesus. But it does not, of course, *prove* that he is.

Toward late afternoon on the Friday of the crucifixion, Orthodox Jews were becoming concerned that the bodies of Jesus and the two thieves might contaminate the Sabbath. The Jewish Sabbath begins at sunset on Friday and continues all through Saturday. They therefore persuaded the Romans to hasten the death and burial of the three crucified men. The method used by the Romans was to break the legs of the victims on the cross. This fact perfectly agrees with what Dr. Barbet said about the cause of death on the cross. Remember that the victim's inability to breathe caused him to shift his weight onto his feet until normal breathing was restored. Now, with the legs broken, the victim would not be able to regain his breath, and death would come sooner. Jesus' legs were not broken; he was already dead. Neither are the Shroud man's legs broken.

As with the crown of thorns, so too the wound in the side increases the chances that it is Jesus on the Shroud. Normally, crucifixion was reserved for the worst criminals: traitors against their country and slaves who had betrayed their masters. After death on the cross it was rare that family and friends came to claim the body. Crucifixion was so horrible a punishment that few people would want to risk being connected to the criminal. So victims were usually thrown into a common grave and there were no mourners. In the case of Jesus, we know that his mother and his followers came to claim the body. In order to assure that he was really dead before handing over the body, and perhaps to stifle any rumors that he might still be alive, the soldier on duty stabbed Jesus in the heart. So the side wound is rare. Jesus had it, and the Shroud man has it.

Even though the Bible is silent about what happened to the Shroud after Easter, there are other documents of an unofficial nature which do point to the

The side wound (boxed area on this picture) seems to be a serious wound, judging by the large amount of blood in this area.

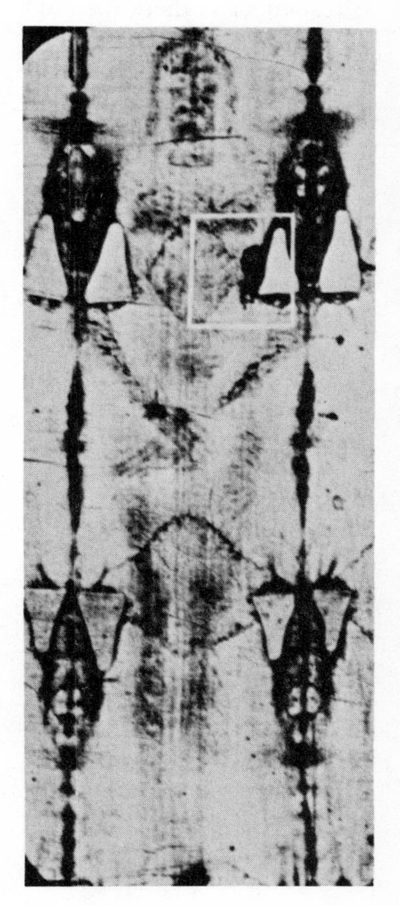

"St. Jerome quoted from the *Gospel of the Hebrews* that after Jesus' resurrection but before he appeared to his brother, James, Jesus gave his sindon (shroud) to 'the servant of the priest.' "

Religious writer Frank C. Tribbe, *Portrait of Jesus?*

"Nowhere in the New Testament is there mention of Christ's shroud having been imprinted with his 'portrait,' or any indication that his burial clothes were even preserved."

Author Joe Nickell, *Inquest on the Shroud of Turin*

Shroud's survival after Easter Sunday. In the second century (about 100-200 A.D.), several accounts were written about the life of Christ. These biographies are similar to the Gospel accounts in the Bible. For various reasons the early Church Fathers did not include them among the "official" texts of the Bible. Some of these writings contain incorrect religious teachings; some are just copies of the Gospels with a few additions. Hence we have called them "unofficial." The usual word for these books is "apocryphal" or "hidden" books. But because they were excluded from the Bible does not mean that they are utterly false. They agree with the Gospels on many points. As books actually written in the second century, they are valuable source materials for that time.

Most importantly, these texts say that Jesus' shroud was removed from the tomb and saved. Writers of the second century, therefore, knew of the existence of this sheet in their own day.

The first of these apocryphal books is called the *Gospel of the Hebrews*. The author is anonymous (unknown) as is the case with all these apocryphal books. We have only fragments from it, for most of it has been lost over the centuries. One key surviving passage says, "After the Lord gave his shroud to the servant of the priest [or of Peter; the actual word is not clear], he appeared to James."

The Acts of Pilate is another apocryphal book of the second century. It states that Pilate and his wife preserved the shroud of Jesus. It suggests that they were sorry for their part in his death and were now Christians.

These two books, along with the *Gospel of Peter, The Acts of Nicodemus,* and *The Gospel of Gamaliel,* show us that second century writers knew about the Shroud in their day. They disagree about who saved it from the tomb, but they agree that it had been saved. The silence of the "official" Biblical stories about the preservation of the shroud is countered by these books.

This tenth century artist's copy of the Edessa cloth is a fresco from the church of St. John at Sakli, Cappadocia. Its shape may be evidence of the frame which could have held the Mandylion.

The Jerusalem Documents

The Shroud record is again silent for nearly two centuries. These are centuries of persecution of Christians. The earliest martyrs died for their faith during this period. The Shroud may have continued to be hidden away for its own protection.

The next reference to it comes in the biography of a young girl named St. Nino. She had visited Jerusalem during the time of Constantine. Constantine (312-337 A.D.) was the first Christian to rule the Roman Empire. It was he who put an end to the religious persecution of Christians. He also decreed that death by crucifixion should be outlawed.

St. Nino took a great interest in the relics of Jesus' Passion (the sad events from the Last Supper on Thursday, through Good Friday, to Easter Sunday). These relics included the nails that pierced his hands and feet, the crown of thorns, the wood of the cross, the sponge with vinegared wine, the lance point that pierced his side, and, of course, his burial sheet. Jesus' shroud, she reported, had been preserved by the wife of Pilate, who then gave it to St. Luke who hid it away. After some time, St. Peter found it and kept it. St. Nino's account is proof that in fourth-century Jerusalem people still knew of the Shroud's existence.

After St. Nino, the plot thickens. There is still

more evidence for the Shroud of Jesus in Jerusalem; but there is also evidence which places the Shroud in the small town of Urfa in southern Turkey (see map). The ancient name of Urfa was Edessa. Here, legend has it, existed a cloth with which Jesus had wiped his face, leaving on it a miraculous portrait. It was known as the Mandylion or the Holy Icon of Edessa. What could this imprinted face cloth have to do with the imprinted body cloth in Turin today?

First let us review the four references to Jesus' sheet in Jerusalem. Then we will turn full attention to the "Edessa connection."

1) Around the year 570 a pilgrim to the Holy Land, Antonius of Placentia, wrote of seeing a cave on the banks of the Jordan River. In it were seven cells, or rooms. In one of the cells was found "the sudarium which was upon Jesus' head."

2) Not much later, St. Braulion of Saragossa, Spain (585-651) also saw in Jerusalem the "linens and sudarium in which the Lord's body was wrapped." He adds something which might be good to keep in mind: "There are events of which the Gospels do not speak . . . such as preserving the burial sheet."

3) Next comes the wording to the "Mozarabic Liturgy." (A liturgy is the "script" of a religious service.) This text was originally written in the sixth century, so it is contemporary with Antonius and Braulion. The lines which intrigue the student of the Shroud read, "Peter ran with John to the sepulcher. He saw the linens and on them the recent *traces* of the death and resurrection." Could this be the first hint that the surviving grave wrapping showed an image?

4) About a hundred years later, around 680, Arculf, a French Bishop, visited Jerusalem. He relates a story he had heard. The sudarium, sometimes called the *linteamen* (linen), was taken from the tomb after the resurrection by a Christian but later fell into the hands of Jews. The Christians wanted it back and

"The more one studies the Gospel record, the more it seems to justify the view . . . that the *sindon* was torn up to form the strip or bands which swathed the corpse."

Shroud Researcher
Father Herbert Thurston

"Any presumption that the body was wrapped *round* in a winding sheet . . . rather like an Egyptian mummy, is read into the texts and has no support in Palestinian burial customs, which the fourth evangelist (John) insists were followed."

Anglican Bishop
John A.T. Robinson

brought their case before the Arab caliph who ruled Jerusalem at the time. He ordered a trial by fire. (The only thing that makes sense in this story is the ending.) The cloth was placed in the fire but wondrously flew out and landed among the Christians. Arculf says that he himself had seen and kissed this linen. It was eight feet long. This is much shorter than the Turin Shroud (14.3 feet), and Arculf does not hint at any image. The only way of identifying Arculf's shroud with that in Turin is to suppose Arculf saw the cloth folded in half: Eight feet is roughly half the size of the Shroud of Turin. It is not so easy to explain the absence of imprint. Wouldn't he have mentioned it if he had seen it?

The historical records placing the Shroud in Jerusalem are not very persuasive. They may refer to some cloth other than the real burial sheet of Jesus. However, they cannot be discounted completely, especially Arculf's story. They do represent part of the Shroud mystery.

Perhaps the reader has been a good detective and noticed a difficulty already. We cannot be certain that the Shroud in Turin today is the same one referred to in these early histories. None of these accounts directly mentions an image. This is part of the ongoing mystery of the Shroud.

Another problem faced by the reader-as-detective is that so many different Greek or Latin words were used for the burial wrappings of Jesus in the early documents. Sometimes the terms are plural and may include the large sheet (*sindon*) plus the head or chin cloth (*sudarium*) and/or the strips of cloth or bandages used to tie or bundle the *sindon* around the body (*othonia*). Sometimes only one of these terms appears and seems to refer to the large sheet. The historical references are as mysterious and confusing as the scientific work. But tracing the history of the Shroud is no less important or intriguing.

Seven

The Edessa Connection

There is a small town in southern Turkey named Urfa. The ancient name of Urfa was Edessa. Here, legend has it, existed a cloth on which Jesus had wiped his face, leaving a miraculous portrait. It was known as the *Mandylion,* or the Holy Icon of Edessa. Can this imprinted face cloth tell us something about the Shroud of Turin?

Ian Wilson, an Oxford University historian, originated a theory, accepted by most scholars today, that the Turin Shroud may have spent nine centuries in Edessa. Wilson's fine book, *The Turin Shroud,* appeared in 1978. The Edessa theory, if true, would explain the Shroud's whereabouts from the crucifixion until 944. This is the greater part of the missing thirteen centuries. But the theory has its own complexities and uncertainties.

Wilson's theory is strengthened by the pollens on the Shroud that come from plants characteristic of the region around Edessa. Also, archaeologists have discovered that Edessa was one of the earliest Christian towns. In the ruins of ancient Edessa, building foundations have been uncovered which may be the remains of the world's first Christian churches.

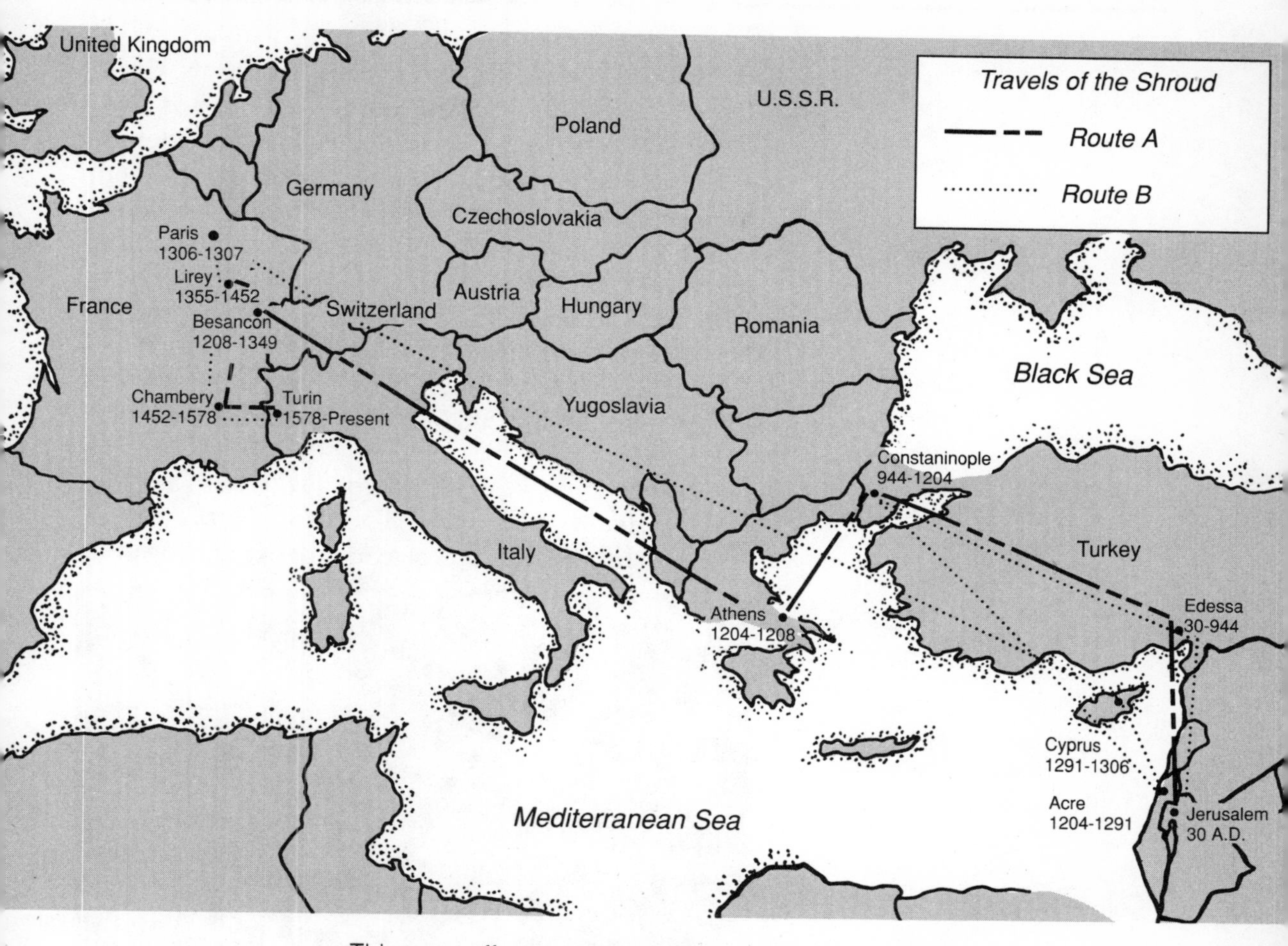

This map offers two possibilities for the route the Shroud may have taken from the time of Jesus' death up to 1578. Both routes trace the cloth's travels from Jerusalem to Edessa to Constantinople. The author formulated route A, which then takes it to Athens, Besancon, Lirey, Chambery and finally Turin. Ian Wilson's theory, route B, shows the Shroud leaving Constantinople, going to Acre, Cyprus, Paris, and then on to Lirey, Chambery, and Turin.

In the decades after the crucifixion of Jesus, Christians were not safe in Jerusalem. The city was troubled by violence between Roman soldiers and Jewish zealots. If these first Christians did have the Shroud, as the apocrypha seem to prove, Jerusalem would not be the safest place in the world to protect it. Neither would Rome, where Nero was already persecuting Christians after 64 A.D. In fact, Christians moved north in great numbers to towns such as Antioch and Edessa. Either town would have been a secure haven for the precious Shroud of Jesus. The evidence points to Edessa.

An apocryphal fourth century text called *The Doctrine of Addai* is the earliest record of a portrait of Jesus in Edessa. In it we read that King Abgar of

St. Catherine's monastery in Sinai owns this tenth century painting of King Abgar holding the Edessa cloth.

Edessa was seriously ill. He had heard of Jesus, the great healer, in Jerusalem. He sent his messenger, Hannan, with a letter requesting that Jesus come to Edessa to heal him. Jesus responded that he was busy with his Father's work and could not come. But Hannan painted Jesus' portrait using "choice" colors and returned to Edessa. Abgar was healed by touching the portrait and kept it with great honor in the palace.

The Abgar story was also told, somewhat differently, by Eusebius, fourth century Bishop of Caesarea (in Palestine). In his version there is no mention of a portrait. He alters another point: He reports that Jesus sent his reply to Abgar in a letter, and it was this letter which cured Abgar and was kept with all honor and care. Other versions mention both a portrait *and* a written letter.

In 594 the historian Evagrius converted the portrait painted with "choice" paints into a portrait miraculously not made by human hands. Describing an attack on Edessa by King Chosroes of Persia in 544, Evagrius tells how the city was saved by the old image of Jesus. The holy cloth had been rediscovered in a niche above the Sacred Gate in the Edessa city walls. It had been deposited there after Abgar's death, when the city came to be ruled by non-Christians. Evagrius writes of this image as if it was well known.

Meanwhile, another historian, Procopius, also described the siege of Edessa by King Chosroes. But in his account there is no hint of a portrait, miraculous or otherwise. Procopius, too, was a contemporary of the events, living in the sixth century. One must choose between the accounts of Evagrius and Procopius.

Still another version of the Abgar story appeared in a work called *The Acts of Thaddeus.* The messenger of Abgar, in this account named Ananias, tried to paint Jesus, but he was unsuccessful. Taking pity on him, Jesus washed and then wiped his face with a cloth "doubled in four." On this towel Jesus left the miraculous "not-made-by-human hands" imprint of

"What is now known as the Shroud of Turin was in the Middle Ages the Mandylion of Edessa and Constantinople."

Author Robert Drews, *In Search of the Shroud of Turin*

"It seems odd that the disciples would let their Lord's shroud go in a disguised form to a city relatively unknown to them."

Historian Steven Runciman, *Cambridge Historical Journal*

Here author Daniel Scavone and Ian Wilson discuss the historical theories surrounding the Shroud of Turin.

his face.

Three details should be noted. First, the word used for "towel" in this version is *sindon,* which is the Greek word for *body* shroud. Second, the towel is *tetradiplon,* "doubled in four." Third, the portrait is now "not made by human hands" (Greek word, *acheiropoietos*). These three clues finally bring us back in touch with the Shroud of Turin. These details are hints that Wilson may have been correct and that the Edessa face cloth may in reality be the Turin Shroud in disguise. What clues support this theory?

Artists' Copies of the Edessa Cloth

The Edessa icon no longer exists as such. However, copies were made by early artists. These copies show a frontal face of Jesus as it should be if it resulted from wiping his face. They show the cloth stretched out and tacked on a wooden frame. The face is seen in a circular central opening. The rest of the towel is covered by a wood frame carved with fairly typical Byzantine decorative designs. This is what those early artists saw, and this is what they copied.

But there is something strange about these copies. Most of them are wide and short. Normally, portraits (like school photos) are tall and narrow. Wilson believes that this cloth (called a *sindon* in the *Acts of Thaddeus*) was always the Shroud, but doubled in four (*tetradiplon*). If this were done with the Turin Shroud, a panel showing only the face would be seen.

Recall the puzzling side strip on the Shroud of Turin described in chapter one. We have no information about why or when this strip of linen was sewn onto one long edge of the Shroud. However, this might be that moment: the side strip centers the image on the Turin Shroud. It would make the face appear in the center of the frame rather than off to one side.

Ian Wilson suggests that the early Christians brought the Shroud with them to Edessa for safety. He also thinks they folded it in that way for two good reasons. First, the body of Jesus was naked. Second, it was horribly bloodied from crucifixion and beatings. These Christians would have known that they could gain few converts by showing pagans the bloody body of "the Savior who could not save himself." The promise of bloody martyrdom is not going to win people over to your group.

Looking at it from another angle, the Edessa face cloth must have been quite large in order to be doubled two times and still allow the face to be seen in its own panel. It would have to be about the size of the Turin Shroud. Look again at the Shroud and notice how the face does seem to be somewhat separated from the chest. If the Shroud were to be folded with only the face showing, one would not know that there was a body hidden behind the folds.

According to Wilson, three centuries passed (about 50-350 A.D.) and the people of Edessa no longer knew what it was that they possessed. It was always the Shroud, but after so long a time people knew it only as a framed face of Jesus, and they forgot how it had come to Edessa. Hence the *Doctrine of Addai,* the first Abgar story, was written in the fourth century in order to explain the coming of a face cloth. It is sad to think that the later people of Edessa probably

The sequence in which the Shroud may have been folded, "doubled-in-four," so that only the face showed.

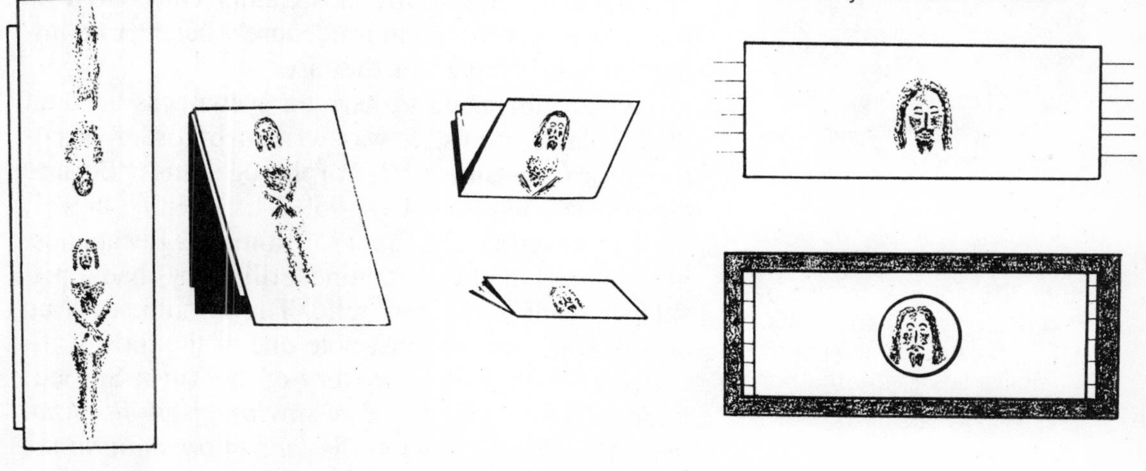

Three Byzantine gold solidi coins. The top two were struck by Justinian II around 692. The lower one was by Constantine VII, about 950. These icons all show similarities to the man on the Shroud.

never knew that their city may have possessed the original burial wrapping with the actual blood of Jesus on it.

The Mandylion Is Rediscovered

Evagrius's account of the Persian siege of 544 attempts to relate how and when the relic came to be rediscovered. It was still in its frame and the people of Edessa probably still thought it was merely Jesus' face-only portrait. This Mandylion, as the Holy Icon of Edessa was called, remained as a protective talisman (good luck charm) in Edessa until 943. In that year, Byzantine Emperor Romanus Lecapenus sent an army to Edessa to get the Mandylion. He wished to add it to the great collection of relics of Jesus which little by little had come to Constantinople. This shows how seriously the Byzantines believed in these relics that were thought to have been connected to Jesus' passion and death 900 years earlier.

After much delay, the Edessa leaders finally turned over their still-framed portrait of Jesus. The arrival of the relic in the capital was marked by a great celebration. It was carried in procession through the streets of the city. The people came out in droves to catch a glimpse of it or touch it. That day, August 15, was honored as the Feast Day of the Holy Face of Jesus in the Greek Orthodox Church calendar. This was apparently the usual procedure whenever an important relic arrived in the city.

We are fortunate to have an eyewitness account of this day's events. It was written by order of co-Emperor Constantine VII Porphyrogenitus ("Born to the Purple") who ruled 912-959. That evening in 944, his scribes wrote, the Emperor Romanus Lecapenus, his two sons, and Constantine (still a boy) had a private showing of the new relic. They would see it up close! And here we must note one of the most critical clues in the entire mystery of the Turin Shroud: *the description of what they saw precisely fits what one sees when looking at the face of the man on the*

Turin Shroud.

Recall that the actual image on the Shroud is very faint. It can be seen only at a distance of ten or more feet. At close range it virtually disappears because the contrast between the imprint and the cloth is so small. Here are the words of this *Narration of Constantine Concerning the Image of Edessa:*

> As for the cause of the image, it is more a moist secretion without colors or art of a painting. And the face is formed on the linen cloth in a way which made the perishable cloth indestructible.
>
> Abgar too had noticed that the likeness "did not consist of earthly colors."

The *Narration of Constantine* contains another description of the Mandylion which may give us a clue that someone noticed blood on the face:

> There is another story. . . . When Christ was about to go voluntarily to death . . . sweat dripped from him like drops of blood. Then they say he took this piece of cloth which we see now from one of the disciples and wiped off the drops of sweat on it.

Importantly, this version of the Mandylion story, which mentions the blood on the face, is a strong clue that the Edessa Mandylion may really have been the Shroud. This idea was reinforced in 1986 by an Italian Shroud scholar named Dr. G. Zaninotto who discovered a Greek manuscript of a sermon by a certain Gregory, archdeacon of Hagia Sophia Church in Constantinople. The sermon was delivered on August 16, 944, the day after the arrival of the Mandylion in the Byzantine capital. As an eyewitness of the events, Gregory gives the names and ranks of those who participated in the celebration. He mentions the crowning of the image with the emperor's crown and the honorary placing of the image on the imperial throne. After reciting the Abgar legend, Gregory says the image was formed by "the perspiration of death on his face." Then comes the most surprising part: he speaks of the side wound and the blood found there.

"The central problem is how 50 square feet of high-grade linen, uniquely bearing a life-size image sacred to Christendom, could have escaped explicit historical notice for thirteen centuries."

Research physicist Marvin Mueller, Los Alamos National Laboratory

"It appears that someone at the very earliest stages of the Shroud's existence mounted and folded the Shroud in such a way that it no longer looked like a shroud . . . this was done in such a clever way that . . . it deceived many generations."

Shroud historian Ian Wilson

Compare this seventeenth century icon of the Mandylion to the Shroud face below. How many similarities do you find?

Here is striking evidence that the Mandylion and Shroud were one and the same object.

More Evidence that the Mandylion Is the Shroud

To this should be added another description of the Mandylion face written around the same time as Constantine's narrative. It is the record of the same evening by Symeon Magister, a tenth century writer in Constantinople. He writes, "The sons of Romanus said that they could see nothing but a faint face. Constantine, however, said that he could make out features such as eyes and ears."

Look at the closeup photograph of the Shroud face. It precisely fits Constantine's and Symeon's remarks: apparent absence of artist's colors, faintness of image, traces of blood.

If this is correct, then the relic brought from Edessa to Constantinople is identical with the Turin Shroud, but folded and framed so as to show only the face. It would then be true that the relic which had been in Edessa for 900 years—since the early days of the Christian faith, and perhaps all the way back to the time of Abgar (that is Jesus' time)—was always the Turin Shroud.

Documents from Constantinople

Once it was placed in the Byzantine treasury with the other relics, we hear little about the Mandylion. However, whenever distinguished visitors came to Constantinople, they were given a tour of the relic collection. Many were so amazed that they wrote accounts of what they had seen. The Mandylion is mentioned in several such lists of relics up to about 1200.

Suddenly, in a list from the year 1157 there appears among the relics the "burial sheet which had wrapped the Lord's body in the tomb." Without the sermon of Gregory and the second version of the *Narration of Constantine* we would be mystified about where this remarkable addition to the collection came from. There is no record of its discovery in any town of the Middle East. There is no celebration, no procession in Constantinople, no annual feast day, as for the other relics. What had been known by Gregory in 944 seems to have been forgotten. The Mandylion remained in its frame, and its true identity as the entire Shroud was forgotten.

In the mid-twelfth century, Ian Wilson theorizes, some caretaker of the relics wished to reframe the Edessa Icon or Mandylion. He undid the tacks, removed the decorative paneling, and took apart the frame. These were very old and not worthy of the towel which it was believed Jesus had touched and upon which he had left his image. Thus, by accident, after 1000 years, that which had been hidden and forgotten behind its mounting—the bloodstained Shroud of Jesus—saw the light of day once more.

The Byzantine church leaders were in a confusion. What about the Mandylion? What should they bring out and honor in procession on its annual holiday? Their solution, according to Wilson, was to make a copy of it. We do know for a fact that a Mandylion continues to be named in most of the tourists' lists after this date (1157).

As for the Shroud, it was obviously preserved in the collection—it is always listed by visitors from this time on. But its chance discovery in the manner described above does seem likely for there is no record of its coming to Constantinople as with other relics and no record of a celebration.

That this might be the way it happened is supported by another set of clues. Around the time of the first reference to a burial shroud among the relics, a new way of representing Jesus began in Byzantine art. It is called the *epitaphios* ("Epitaph" or "burial") or *threnos* ("mourning") scene. These pictures are paintings or woven tapestries. In them, Jesus is shown lying dead upon a large shroud. His hands are folded just as they are on the Turin Shroud. In some exam-

A face of Jesus is embossed on this silver bowl found at Homs, Syria. The bowl is dated to the sixth century. Again we see a resemblance to the Shroud face, suggesting that these early icons used the Shroud as a model.

"The nearby Dead Sea Qumran Community graves have been extensively excavated, and they have found skeletons in the exact position of the Man on the Shroud: stretched out flat on the back, face up, hands over the pelvic region."

Religious writer Frank C. Tribbe, *Portrait of Jesus?*

"The crossed-hands pose on the shroud of Turin looks suspiciously like a concession to medieval prudery. In Jewish burial practices, the hands are always crossed on the chest, leaving the genitals exposed."

Reverend David Sox, former secretary of the British Society for the Turin Shroud

Opposite page: The early fifteenth-century wooden sculpture of Christ, from Lucerne, Switzerland, shows the hands crossed exactly as the man in the Shroud has his hands.

ples Christ is depicted unclothed, as is the man on the Shroud. Previously Christ had been shown on the cross or being taken down and wrapped as a mummy. It is quite possible that the awareness of the long fourteen-foot sheet in Constantinople inspired this new art. This artistic style of showing Jesus coincides with the first references to the burial sheet in the relic lists.

Other Documents Support Wilson's Theory

Other texts going back to the same period lend support to this theory that the Edessa Icon, the face cloth, was discovered at some time to be the Shroud of Jesus.

Around 1140 Ordericus Vitalis, a monk from England, was writing his *History of the Church.* When he came to an important event of his own day, the capture of Edessa in the First Crusade, he retold the Abgar story. In his version the story takes on a dramatic new twist: Jesus sent Abgar the letter and the linen "which showed to those who saw it the appearance and *size of the body* of the Lord." This text seems to be saying that more and more people thought that the object which had come to Constantinople from Edessa was a body image and not just a facial image on cloth.

Also from the twelfth century we have a sermon which retells yet again the Edessa story. In it Jesus' supposed letter is quoted: "If you wish to see my human face, here is a linen on which you can see not only the features of my face but the stature of my whole body divinely formed." The sermon continues: Jesus "then lay down full length on a linen cloth white as snow and, wonderful to behold, by the act of God, the glorious features of the Lord and noble stature of his body were imprinted on it."

This sermon is a twelfth century copy of a sermon of Pope Stephen III, originally delivered in 769. In the original sermon, Jesus' letter mentioned only the Edessa towel with its miraculous facial image and not that of the entire body. Clearly the twelfth century copyist changed it according to information he had. He knew there was in Constantinople a sheet with Jesus' entire body depicted on it.

In about 1212 Gervase of Tilbury repeats almost word for word this latest version. He too adds a detail which he claims came from "reliable ancient archives": Jesus is described as being crucified *unclothed.*

The final document we must consider was written by the *Skeuophylax* or Keeper of the Imperial Treasury, Nicholas Mesarites. He was a priest from an important Constantinople family. In 1201 he was guardian of the relics in the Pharos Chapel. In that year a revolution took place in the palace. The Pharos Treasury was in danger of being looted. Nicholas tells us how he threw himself in front of the door and delivered a powerful speech reminding the crowd of the holiness of the place and its contents. He named each relic. "Here too," he continued, "the Lord is resurrected anew and the *sudarium* and burial linens are proof of it. . . . These linens still smell of myrrh and they resist corruption since they enveloped the indefinable, naked and embalmed corpse of the Lord after the Passion."

As caretaker of the relics, Mesarites must have had intimate knowledge of his treasures. His words are hints that he saw the nude image on the burial sheet. This is the last clear reference to the Shroud in the Pharos Treasury, which was the relic repository in the Imperial Palace in Constantinople.

Taken together, these texts are evidence that people from the twelfth century on knew of the existence of a large cloth with the full image of Christ's naked body on it. The image was very faint and stained with blood. While they seem to be referring to the Shroud of Turin, the texts are vague. Since we cannot be certain if they refer to the Shroud, the mystery is not yet solved to our complete satisfaction. More clues are yet to come. And more controversy.

Eight

The Shroud Leaves Constantinople

The last records of the Shroud in Constantinople have to do with how it came to leave the capital city. Almost all Shroud historians now accept that somehow the Shroud of Jesus was in Constantinople from 944 on (if it came from Edessa) or from some less precisely known date (if it came from Jerusalem).

The Fourth Crusade

In 1203 the peace of Constantinople was again shattered by the coming of the French, Italian, and Flemish (Dutch) knights of the Fourth Crusade. This crusade was one of the worst scandals in the history of Christianity.

From their arrival in Constantinople in spring of 1203 until April 1204, the crusading knights waited for the Byzantine emperor to provide the funds to pay for their transport to the Holy Land for the war against the Moslem Turks. During this time the knights had opportunities to tour the rich churches of the capital. They noticed the great wealth concentrated in the city. There were more relics there, they wrote, than in all the other Christian cities of Europe combined.

When the emperor broke his promise of financial support, the knights became angry and frustrated.

This etching depicts the battle of Poitiers in 1356. Here crusader and knight Geoffroy de Charny was killed. His possession of the Shroud remains a mystery.

They had waited all winter. They remembered the treasures they had seen in the churches. Instead of crusading against the Turks and winning back the Holy Land, the Christian knights pillaged the greatest Christian city in the East.

The capture of Constantinople by the crusaders took place on April 12, 1204. For three days the knights were out of control. The two imperial palaces were secured by the crusader leaders so their treasuries were not ransacked. But the great church of Hagia Sophia certainly was. Its precious gold and silver religious vessels became the property of the crusaders. They stole everything of value. The four life-size gilded bronze horses which even today adorn St. Mark's Church in Venice came from Constantinople during the Fourth Crusade.

One of the French knights left a most important record. Robert of Clari was an ordinary knight. He was not among the leaders of the Crusade. During

The church of Hagia Sophia as it looks today.

the months of waiting he visited all the important churches of the city. He was quite impressed, especially with Hagia Sophia and the church of Our Lady of Blachernae. In the latter church he reported seeing the "*sydoines (sindon*, shroud) in which our Lord was wrapped, and which each Friday stood straight up, so that it was possible to see the figure of our Lord. But when the city was taken, no one, whether Greek or French, knew what became of it." This is the text which almost all writers quote as proof that the Turin Shroud was in Constantinople in 1204.

"No one, either Greek or French, ever knew what became of this sydoines [shroud] after the city was taken."

Crusader Robert de Clari, 1204

What Happened to the Shroud?

What *did* become of the shroud which Clari saw? Why was it in Blachernae exposed to the view of tourists such as Clari and not in the Pharos Treasury with the other relics? To answer the second question, perhaps the Byzantines were hoping that the Shroud would save their city from the crusaders. In Edessa, the cloth had served this protective purpose.

"But, of course, someone knew. This might just have been the story the crusader hierarchy wanted believed, so that the Shroud could be quietly diverted—possibly to the Templar treasury."

Religious writer Frank C. Tribbe, *Portrait of Jesus?*

As for the first question, the answer is simple: The Shroud disappeared again for 151 years until Geoffroy I de Charny deposited it in his church at Lirey, France, in 1355 or so. However, where the Turin Shroud is concerned, nothing is simple. As the reader might suspect by now, the last phase of the mystery of the Shroud is about to begin. It concerns the Shroud's whereabouts for 151 years, from 1204 to 1355.

The Crusaders Establish a Latin Government

Before we present the main theories, let us see what happened in Constantinople. The crusaders completely controlled the city from 1204 until 1261. They elected their own Latin Byzantine emperors. The most important were Henry of Hainaut in Flanders (ruled 1205-16) and Baldwin II (ruled 1228-61). Greek Orthodox priests and bishops were replaced with Latin Roman clergy from Europe. Nicholas Mesarites, the caretaker of the relics, for example, surely lost his job in 1204.

Site of Blachernae, Constantinople, where Crusader Robert of Clari reported seeing the burial shroud of Jesus.

The Greek imperial government was thrown out. In Nicaea, across the Bosporus, the strait that separates Asia from Europe, the Greek leaders set up a new Byzantine government-in-exile. Sometime soon after 1204, Nicholas Mesarites was made Archbishop of Ephesus, a chief city of the Nicaean government. The Greeks waited their chance to regain Constantinople as their rightful capital. This they did, but not until 1261.

In the meantime, French and Italian knights conquered and ruled the major provinces of the Byzantine Empire in Greece. Othon de La Roche, a knight from Burgundy, was made Lord of Athens and Thebes. He was a vassal of Boniface of Montferrat, an Italian knight and new King of Thessalonika in the north of Greece. European-type feudalism was introduced into the new Latin Byzantine Empire. European knights ruled in almost all of the provinces of the old Greek Byzantine Empire.

But there were great pressures on the Latin Byzantine Empire, especially under its last ruler, Baldwin II. The Greek province of Epirus resisted the Latin takeover. It remained under the rule of Greek nobles. The old Byzantine emperors at Nicaea grew stronger and stronger. Baldwin II was always short of money to supply his armies and defend his territory.

He began pawning off the precious relics of Jesus' Passion. Bankers of Venice lent him money on Jesus' Crown of Thorns and some minor relics. Back in France, King Louis IX was shocked that these relics were being "put in hock." He repaid the loan and took possession of the Crown of Thorns. Thus the Crown of Thorns left Constantinople and came to reside in Paris, safe for the time being. (King Louis IX is also known as St. Louis for religious activities such as this.)

Baldwin II also sent relics to the castles of the Knights Templar in return for other loans. This group was an order of fighting monks who had fought in earlier crusades. Their fortified castles were known to be impossible to capture. Much wealth was stored in these castles for safety. They could protect Baldwin's relics until he repaid his loans.

The Templars May Have Kept the Shroud

Ian Wilson put forth a theory which many followers of Shroud history have accepted. Since there is so little evidence about what happened to it after Clari's report, Wilson feels the Shroud may have been deposited with the Templars in return for a loan to Baldwin II. In one of their castles, unpublicized, it remained silent and safe for many years.

But not forever. Wilson draws our attention to the disbanding of the Templars in 1307. At that time the Order was brought to trial by the King of France—Philip the Fair—and Pope Clement V. Why were these proceedings brought against such a courageous and honorable order of knights? There were several charges. Among them was the accusation that the Templars were worshipping an idol at their most secret religious services. During the trial some Templars testified that in the dark the idol seemed to be a head with a reddish beard. Testimonies varied, but many of them seem to point to the Shroud face as the object of the secret worship of the Templars.

If this is so, then the "idol" the Templars were worshipping may have been the Shroud, again folded. It would be one explanation of the whereabouts of the Shroud after Clari's statement that no one knew what became of it.

As a climax to his theory Wilson reports that in 1314 the leaders of the Templars were burned at the stake for heresy (in this case worshipping idols). Among them was a man named Geoffroy de Charnay. This Templar may have been an ancestor of the owner of the Shroud in Lirey, France. Perhaps, Wilson says, this Templar had hidden the Shroud (the Templar "idol") in his family's castle, where it remained for another 41 years. Then, in 1355 it was dis-

"Where the Mandylion/Shroud was between the years 1204 and ca. 1355 is not known."

Author Robert Drews, *In Search of the Shroud*

"It was the Templars who had the Shroud, and . . . it was in the family of one of the masters of the order that it found its new home."

Shroud historian Ian Wilson, *The Shroud of Turin*

played at Lirey.

One of the artifacts that Wilson believes supports the Templar theory is a wooden panel from Templecombe, England, a Templar headquarters. The panel is decorated with a face of Jesus that is strikingly similar to the Shroud face. Wilson believes it is an artist's copy of the Templar idol.

In 1987 Shroud scholar Rex Morgan came up with an astonishing theory that may shed some light on this remarkable panel. Morgan thinks that the panel may have been the lid of a chest that held the Shroud. Perhaps at the time the Templars were being disbanded, they had shipped it to England. Geoffroy then may have acquired it during the year 1350 when he was a prisoner in England.

Othon de La Roche

Another theory of what happened to the Shroud after the Fourth Crusade is that Othon de La Roche brought it with him to Athens. Othon became one of the prominent leaders of the crusaders and was made Lord of Athens in 1204. If the Shroud was in Athens, Othon was the one person among the crusaders who was in an important enough position to have obtained the Shroud. There are two documents in support of this theory, though they do not mention Othon by name. First is a letter from Theodore of Epirus to Pope Innocent III (Pope, 1198-1216) complaining that Constantinople was being stripped of its wealth and its holy relics by the crusaders. Theodore singled out the Shroud of Jesus which he said was taken to Athens. The letter is dated August 1, 1205, about a year after Robert of Clari says the Shroud disappeared from Constantinople.

A second document, dated in 1207, again does not mention Othon by name, but may also place the Shroud in Athens. Nicholas of Otranto, a bilingual interpreter between Greeks and Europeans in Constantinople, wrote that he had seen the Shroud with his own eyes. He wrote elsewhere that he had been

Templar Geoffroy de Charny and the Templar's Grand Master, Jacques de Molay, are being burned at the Stake in 1314.

in Athens in 1206.

What Othon may have done with the Shroud or where he sent it is another area of controversy. From Othon, the Shroud possibly went to the Templars—somehow. This would blend well with Wilson's strong Templar theory.

It is also possible that by about 1208 Othon had shipped the Shroud to his father, Pons de La Roche, who turned it over to Bishop Amadeus de Tramelai for safekeeping in St. Stephen's Cathedral in Besançon, France. This town is not far from Othon's estates in Burgundy, and it is only a relatively short distance from Lirey, the first home of the Turin Shroud.

Is there any evidence for this set of events? Could the Shroud of Turin ever have been in Besançon? Are there any serious arguments against this "Besançon theory"? The answer is "yes" to all three questions.

The evidence in favor of the Shroud having been in Besançon begins with the claims of the town that the Shroud was there since the 1200s. The Besançon claim should be taken seriously since no other place or group claimed to have the Shroud between 1208 and 1355. (Recall that the Templars kept total silence

This wooden panel exhibits a face of Christ, very like that of the Shroud. Found in 1945 at Templecombe, England, where there was a Knights Templar community, the panel is dated to the late thirteenth or early fourteenth century.

about their idol and *never* mentioned having the Shroud.)

Also around 1750, a handwritten document was placed in the Besançon City Library. It was written anonymously. It is called MS 826. It consists of arguments in favor of and against the Besançon theory. The pro argument says that Othon sent the Shroud to his father, Pons, who gave it to the Bishop Amadeus. It names three medieval writers who stated this fact. These sources have not been found; perhaps they no longer exist. The other part of the manuscript denies that the Shroud was ever in Besançon.

The Shroud may have originally been kept privately in the residence of Bishop Amadeus. But at some time, according to this theory, he deposited it in the Cathedral of St. Stephen. This cathedral was badly damaged by fire in 1349. The Shroud disappeared. Everyone thought it had been destroyed in the fire.

Six years later, today's Turin Shroud appeared in nearby Lirey. The history of the Lirey-Chambery-Turin Shroud is so well established from 1355 to the present day that after 1349 we know the Shroud of Turin was not in Besançon.

Is the Besancon Shroud the Real Shroud?

Despite this documentation, in 1375 the new bishop of Besançon announced that their old shroud had been found! He said it had somehow survived the fire. This Besançon shroud was tested by being placed on a dead body. The dead man was said to have miraculously revived. The people of Besançon believed that this was their original shroud, the burial wrapping of Jesus sent by Othon from Athens.

Painted copies of this shroud survive today. They show Jesus only from the front. There is no back (or dorsal) body, as on the Turin Shroud. These copies are why some Shroud scholars disagree with the Besançon theory and claim it was never in Besançon. Because these painted copies do not resemble the Shroud of Turin, some Shroud scholars argue, the Besançon shroud is not the Turin Shroud. Therefore, the Turin Shroud was never in Besançon.

There is one possibility that these scholars neglect, however. The original Besançon shroud of 1349 may have indeed been the Turin Shroud, while the one presented to the people of Besançon in 1375 was different. It may even be the painted shroud which Bishop d'Arcis's artist had admitted painting. Unfortunately, this cloth was shredded into bandages in 1794 during the French Revolution. Also destroyed were many church records in Besançon, including practically all contemporary records dealing with their alleged shroud from 1208 to 1349.

If the 1375 Besançon cloth was the same one that had been there before the fire, why would they need to test it by placing it on a dead body? Is it possible that in 1375 (26 years after the fire of 1349), there was no one alive who knew what the original Besançon shroud looked like and could identify it? This must be the reason that the new one had to be tested.

If the pre-fire Besançon cloth was the Shroud that came into the possession of Geoffroy I de Charny we

"Othon de la Roche received it [the shroud] as part of his recompense upon the fall of the city and sent it to his father in France. His father gave it to the local bishop, who placed it in the Besançon Cathedral."

Reverends Patrick O'Connell and Charles Carty, *The Holy Shroud and Four Visions*

"This suggestion answers a few questions, but seems to be largely one of speculation and is replete with obvious weaknesses—notably, the thought that a relic of such great value would be given to Othon 'as part of his recompense.' "

Religious writer Frank C. Tribbe, *Portrait of Jesus?*

can't say exactly how he got it. However, the distance from Besançon to Lirey is only about 160 miles. Documents do place the Constantinople Shroud in Besançon through Othon. Altogether this seems the shortest and most direct route from Constantinople to Lirey.

The de Vergy Family in Besancon

One additional note has not been fully explored by the historians: it is that the family of Jeanne de Vergy was very prominent in Besançon. Jeanne was Geoffroy I's second wife and widow. She was also the great, great, great, great granddaughter of Othon de La Roche. It may turn out to be the case that *she,* and not Geoffroy, had the Shroud and deposited it in the church at Lirey. The clue might be that Bishop Henry of Poitiers praised Geoffroy I in the one surviving letter. Perhaps his investigation into the Shroud to which Bishop d'Arcis referred took place after Geoffroy was dead. Perhaps the inquest was directed at Jeanne de Vergy, who brought the Shroud with her from the ashes of the fire in St. Stephen's Cathedral in Besançon.

"It is beyond belief that so staggering a discovery (of the 14-foot Shroud folded behind the Edessa face) would have been passed over by all our literary sources."

Historian Averil Cameron

The Besançon theory is by far the best documented of all the theories on the Shroud between 1204 and 1355. Still, many Shroud scholars have disagreed with it. They use three main arguments. First, Shroud scholar Paul Vignon searched for the three documents named in MS 826. He could not find them in the libraries where they were supposed to be. This objection carries little weight. Vignon searched in the 1930s for handwritten records named in 1750, but dating back to the 1200s. It is not surprising that he could not find them.

"Knights and churchmen who returned to the West with stolen relics [were] greeted with adulation. . . . But no one brought to light the Mandylion/Shroud. . . . If, therefore, the cloth survived . . . it 'went underground' in a way that has never previously been identified."

Shroud historian Ian Wilson

The second objection is that the still surviving early records of the city of Besançon and the records of its churches do not refer to Othon de La Roche or the Shroud. This second argument can be answered also. Very few records of Besançon survive from the time before 1349. Many church records were lost in the fire of that year. The French Revolution of 1789 caused even more church records to be destroyed, including practically all older records dealing with the city's alleged shroud from 1208 to 1349, the crucial years. Today the official town records of Besançon go back only to 1418, and even these are not complete. The painted post-1375 cloth was shredded into bandages by the revolutionaries in the year 1794, so it can no longer be inspected. It is likely that records pertaining to it were sought out and destroyed as well.

Third, opponents of the Besançon theory have argued that the post-1375 Besançon shroud, which was certainly painted, is evidence that the Shroud was never in Besançon. But this argument does not prove that the pre-1349 Shroud could not have been in Besançon from 1208 to 1349.

As the case stands, Besançon seems the best of several choices as the home of the Turin Shroud between 1208 and 1349. It bears repeating that of all the candidates that have been proposed (the Templars and Templecombe, Germany, the Toucy family), only Besançon has actually claimed the Shroud; the others are all, without exception, the well-reasoned products of modern scholars. If there are too few documents attesting to the Shroud being in Besançon, there are NO documents placing the Shroud anywhere else.

Epilogue

Radiocarbon Dating: The Final Chapter?

We have seen that the Shroud has been tested and studied by many different scientists and historians and still it is as much a puzzle as ever. But there was one more test that remained to be done: to attempt to learn the date of the Shroud by the Carbon-14 (C-14) method. This process has proved to be successful in determining the dates of objects found by archaeologists digging at ancient sites. Any object which was once living (organic), such as the flax plant which provided the linen of the Shroud, can be dated by the C-14 method if it is under 50,000 years old.

The principle behind the C-14 method is fairly simple. Every living thing (animal, plant, person) receives ordinary Carbon-12 and radioactive C-14 from the atmosphere. When the living thing dies it stops taking in new carbon. C-14, being unstable, begins to change to C-12. In about 5730 years half of the C-14 in the once-living wood, cloth, or bone will be gone. In another 5730 years half of what is left will have disintegrated, 5730 years later and half of what is still left will also have disintegrated, and so on. Thus we say that C-14 has a "half-life" of 5730 years. Experts hoped that by performing the C-14 test on the Shroud

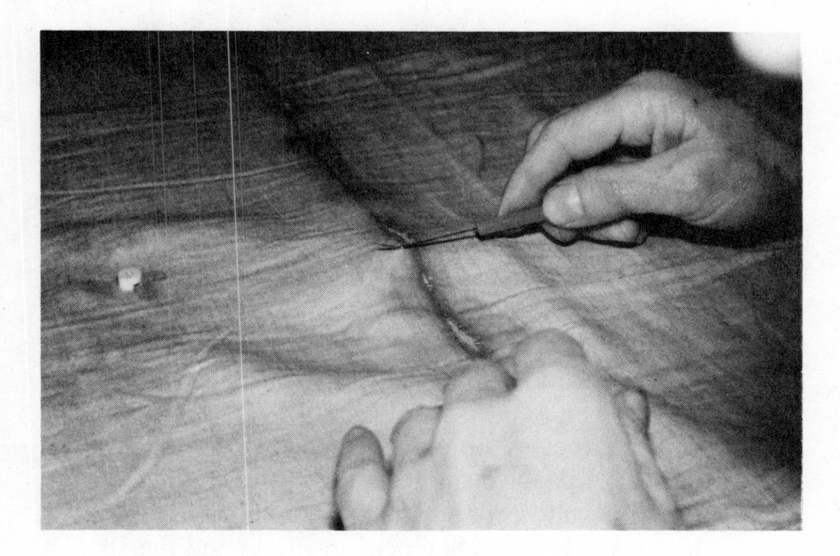

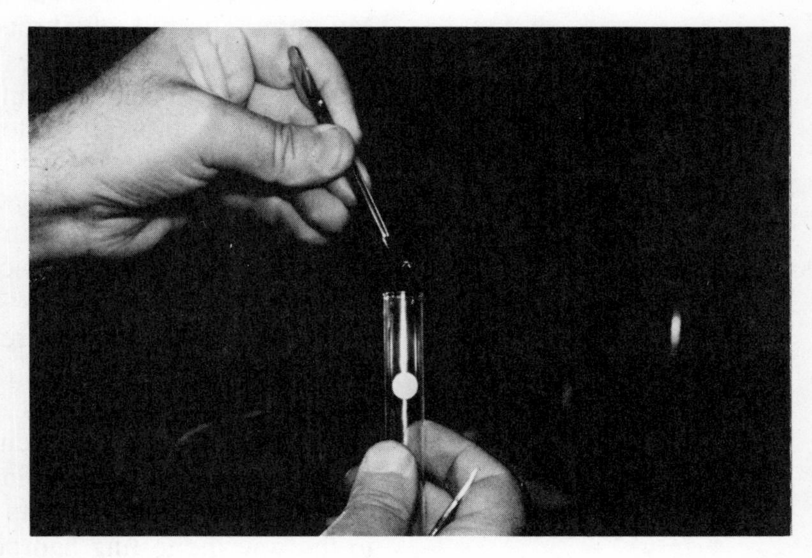

In the top photo scientists take a small sample from the Shroud in 1978. The bottom picture shows the sample being stored in a sterile test tube for testing. In a similar way the sections used in Carbon-14 dating were removed.

of Turin, the test would show the age of the cloth within thirty to two hundred years.

As the test was planned, some C-14 specialists were pessimistic that it could produce an accurate date. They feared that too much contamination had occurred over the centuries. In the case of the Shroud, C-14 transfers from fourteenth, fifteenth, or even twentieth century hands could spoil the reading. Other C-14 experts believed that the cloth could be cleansed of its contamination and the test would give an accurate date for the Shroud. But all agreed that C-14 was not infallible.

Nevertheless, on April 21, 1988, three pieces about the size of postage stamps were cut from the Shroud. The removal was done under the authority of the Pontifical Academy of Sciences in Rome and the British Museum. The bits of Shroud material were hand-delivered to representatives of the University of Arizona, Oxford University in England, and the Swiss Federal Institute of Technology at the University of Zurich. The labs were also given bits of material from other "dummy" cloths whose dates were known. None of the pieces was labeled so that, theoretically at least, the labs could not know which pieces were from the Shroud.

In September 1988, the results were leaked to the press. The Shroud had been carbon-dated to a time around 1350.

Scientists whose research had seemed to support the Shroud's authenticity immediately challenged the C-14 findings. They came up with several objections to the way the testing had been carried out.

They argued that the three labs had been given pieces of cloth taken from a much handled, much contaminated corner of the Shroud. Since only threads were needed, different parts of the Shroud could and should have been included, such as the "pristine" material next to the charred areas under the patches. Another major objection was that all three labs had agreed to use the same newly developed and relatively untested cleansing solvent. Since the contamination from centuries of handling is the most important obstacle to an accurate C-14 date, this procedure seemed to critics to be extremely careless.

The C-14 tests, therefore, did not put an end to the controversy over the Shroud. In fact, the mystery of the famous cloth was even more profound than before. As Luigi Gonella, scientific advisor to the Archbishop of Turin noted, there remained the question of how the image was formed. Also, how could one explain the numerous artistic and historical references which seemed to point to the Shroud as the genuine burial cloth of Jesus? How could one explain the fact that early portraits of Jesus seem to contain features found on the face of the man of the Shroud? How did pollens from the Holy Land get onto the Shroud? How shall we explain Constantine VII's description of the Edessa Mandylion in 944 as a "moist secretion not made with artists' paints," a description which precisely describes the Shroud? If the Shroud was really the burial wrapping of some person centuries later than Jesus, why has it not disintegrated as burial clothing does if left on the corpse for more than thirty-six hours?

The questions surrounding Christianity's greatest relic did not end in 1988. As with all the other tests, theories, and documents, C-14 has added but one more piece to the great puzzle of the Shroud of Turin.

"We can conclude for now that the shroud image is that of a real human form or a scourged, crucified man. It is not the product of an artist. The bloodstains are composed of hemoglobin and also give a positive test for serum albumin. The image is an ongoing mystery and until further chemical studies are made . . . the problem remains unsolved."

STURP, Summary of Official Statement

"The Shroud of Turin is either the most awesome and instructive relic of Christ in existence . . . or it is one of the most ingenious, unbelievably clever products of the human mind and hand on record. It is one or the other. There is no middle ground."

Shroud researcher John Walsh

Books for Further Exploration

Dan Scavone particularly recommends the following books and articles for readers interested in learning more about the Shroud of Turin.

John Heller, *Report on the Shroud of Turin.* Boston: Houghton Mifflin, 1983.

Thomas Humber, *The Sacred Shroud.* New York: Pocket Books, 1977.

Joe Nickell, *Inquest on the Shroud.* Buffalo: Prometheus, 1983.

Ian Wilson, *The Shroud of Turin.* New York: Image Books, 1979.

Ian Wilson, *The Mysterious Shroud.* Garden City, New York: Doubleday & Company, 1986.

Periodicals

Natalie Angier, "Unraveling the Shroud of Turin," *Discover,* October 1982.

Frank W. Martin, "The Shroud of Turin," *People,* vol. 10, no. 22, November 27, 1978.

Newsweek, September 18, 1978.

Kenneth F. Weaver, "The Mystery of the Shroud," *National Geographic,* June 1980.

Additional Bibliography

Barbara Culliton, "The Mystery of the Shroud of Turin Challenges 20th-Century Science," *Science,* vol. 201, July 21, 1978.

Walter McCrone, "Light Microscopical Study of the Turin Shroud, I, II, and III," *The Microscope,* nos. 3 and 4, 1980 and no. 1, 1981.

Samuel Pellicori and Mark Evans, "The Shroud of Turin Through the Microscope," *Archaeology,* no. 34, January-February 1981.

Daniel C. Scavone, "The Shroud in Constantinople: The Documentary Evidence," *Byzantinische Zeitschrift,* vol. 97.1, 1988.

Michael Thomas, "First Polaroid in Palestine: The Shroud of Turin." *Rolling Stone,* December 28, 1978.

For Ongoing Developments

Shroud News, six issues per year, available from The Runciman Press, Box 86, P.O., Manly, 2095, N.S.W., Australia.

Shroud Spectrum International, quarterly journal of the Shroud, available from Indiana Center for Shroud Studies, R.R. 3, Box 557, Nashville, Indiana 47448.

Free catalogues from the Holy Shroud Guild, 294 East 150th Street, Bronx, New York 10451.

Chronology

About 30 AD	Crucifixion of Christ. Joseph of Arimathea buys a burial wrapping for the body.
30-943	The Shroud of Jesus is either in Jerusalem where travelers refer to it, or in Edessa, where there is a history of a towel bearing Jesus' portrait. Edessa is the more likely location. The "portrait" may be the burial Shroud, folded and framed.
944	The Edessa portrait (the Shroud) is taken to Constantinople by force.
About 1157	Jesus' burial wrapping is first mentioned in the Constantinople relic lists. Perhaps the portrait towel has been unfolded for reframing and discovered to be a large burial sheet.
1204	Robert of Clari, French crusader, reports seeing Jesus' burial cloth with image in Constantinople. Last certain reference to the Shroud in Constantinople.
1204-1355	Disputed centuries. Shroud is hidden without any positive documentation. Either it is in a castle of the Knights Templar, or it is somewhere else in the Middle East, or it is in the French town of Bescançon.
1355-57	First absolute date for the Turin Shroud. Shroud is placed in a church at Lirey, France, by Geoffroy I de Charny or by his widow, Jeanne de Vergy.
1357-88	Shroud is removed from the church to a Charny castle for safekeeping during the Hundred Years' War or because the Bishop, of Troyes, Henry de Poitiers, ordered it.

1389 Bishop d'Arcis of Troyes complains to the Pope that Geoffroy II de Charny and the Lirey clergy are deceiving the public with a fake shroud that an artist had admitted painting.

1452 Marguerite de Charny, daughter of Geoffroy II, sells the Shroud to the family of Savoy. Savoys keep ownership until 1983.

1532 Fire in the Savoy cathedral at Chambery, France, damages the Shroud.

1578 Savoys move to Turin, Italy, with their Shroud, which remains there to the present day.

Index

Picture Credits

Daniel Scavone, 7, 82, 92
Vernon Miller, © 1978, 8, 9, 29, 38, 39, 42, 43, 45, 47, 49, 51, 52, 54, 58, 62, 66, 86
Biblioteque Nationale, Paris, 13
Wellcome Institute Library, London, 14
Photo courtesy the National Museums, Paris, 15
Francis L. Filas, S.J., courtesy Father Adam Otterbein, 16, 18, 32, 37, 64, 94
Don Bosco Multimedia, 21, 25 bottom, 26 bottom, 27, 69, 71, 72
Courtesy John Walsh, 22, 23
Patricia Sides, 24, 25 top, 26 top, 83
Mary Ahrndt, 31, 79
Courtesy Joe Nickell, 34, 35
© 1978 Barrie M. Schwortz. All rights reserved. 40, 46, 103
Courtesy Dr. Walter McCrone, 55, 56, 61
From The Mysterious Shroud by Ian Wilson. © 1986 Ian Wilson. Used by permission of Ian Wilson and Doubleday, a division of Bantam, Doubleday, Dell, Publishing Group, Inc.
Courtesy Dr. Alan Whanger, 84
British Museum, 91, 97

About the Author

Daniel Scavone was raised in Chicago, Illinois. He first became interested in the Shroud of Turin as a child when he watched Good Friday television specials about it. As an adult, his fascination with the Shroud was coupled with questions about its authenticity. Now, after many years of research and a number of published articles on the topic, Daniel still finds the Shroud one of the most astonishing mysteries of our time.

Daniel holds a Ph.D. and is a professor of ancient and modern history at the University of Southern Indiana in Evansville. He has been awarded three National Endowment for the Humanities fellowships.

When he's not teaching, Daniel enjoys tennis, jogging, and ice hockey, and is a member of the Evansville Philharmonic Chorus.